The Seven Laws of Nature
Nature's Laws to Successful Living
3rd Edition

(The Seven Laws of Nature Series)
Part One:

By

Dr. Mushtaq H. Jaafri

ISBN: 1-4033-0611-7

This book is printed on acid free paper.

1stBooks - rev. 03/25/02

Contents

The following table of contents is included to give you instant access to key concepts.

How to Use this Book
(Three Step Plan)

Before you read a chapter, set aside a quiet time and place where you can study without interruption. First, examine the chapter headlines to preview what will be covered. Then, assess your knowledge by instantly recalling what you learned.

As you read a chapter, use a marking pencil to highlight important concepts and ideas. If you don't yet understand a law or if you have a question, write it in the margin, so that you can go back and review the chapter. Because the chapters are fairly short, you'll probably read them quickly. Right afterwards, review the passages you highlighted. Ask yourself if you understand the concepts presented. Then, put the law into effect by making a commitment to take the steps at the end of each chapter.

Next, immediately start thc following law. Do not skip around because the material is designed to be a companion in the continual process of change and growth. Master each law, step-by-step, because it is organized incrementally and with suggestions for application at the end of each law. So you can study and focus on any law as you are ready. I suggest that you shift the mind-set of your own involvement in this material from the role of a mere passive learner to that of a teacher.

Remember the best way to learn something is by teaching it to someone else. You'll not only remember better what you read, but your perception will deepen and expand. Read this whole book as if I were your personal friend and I was writing to you, and *You* alone. Learn and then *live* by The Seven Laws Of Nature. You will surely enjoy Heaven on Earth. You can get the most out of this book by following this three-step plan.

Acknowledgments

So many people influenced this book that it would be impossible to mention them all. But I must say special thanks to Abida K. Jaafri my wife, and four children, Lilah, Mustafa, Murtaza, and Mujtaba, for their unshakable faith and support and *accepting* me the way I am and ***NOT*** the way I should be. My wife and children have given me MORE than they received, in ways only a spouse or a father can truly know.

To Dr. Deepak Chopra for his permission, through his attorney in New York City Mr. Jonathan D. Reichman, to adopt "The Seven Laws of Nature" as my alternative title for the second edition of the book.

To Dr. Gayle F. Arrowood for her editing of all three manuscripts, for helping me refine and test the material in several contexts. There can be no better person qualified to write the forward for this book than Dr. Gayle F. Arrowood. I'm grateful for her integrity, sense of quality and her excellent suggestions for helping me understand the difference between writing and speaking.

My very special thanks to Timothy E. Jacobs, President of 1st book Library, for helping me create an ebook for the Internet. I thank God there is a service available for new authors to promote their work on the Internet as well as through the regular channels. I can now realize why it took twenty five years for my mission to start a new cultural transformation in society to materialize because the Internet was not invented yet. And finally, to all my new Internet readers, I'm indeed grateful for your courage and commitment to a vision that is awesome, inspiring, lofty, noble and self-transforming.

Forward

Dr. Mushtaq H. Jaafri is the kind of person who can simplify concepts that are otherwise difficult to assimilate. When you know his full story, however, it will become crystal clear that what he has done to achieve outstanding results is the same thing you can do. He has used his God-given talents and abilities to their maximum potentials and has pursued his desire to share these Nature's Laws to successful living with as many people as possible with dedication, a vision of the potential that is God's gift to every man or woman. He has pursued that dream with single-minded courage and unflagging energy.

I've known Dr. Mushtaq H. Jaafri for many years. I had the privilege and the honor of reviewing and editing both of his manuscripts of The Seven Laws of Nature series. The philosophy and guidelines presented here are timeless. Although the work may be judged philosophical, it is also very pragmatic.

If you seek spiritual growth, this series of books must be read, digested, and reread. They offer more than the usual fix-it books, because they deal with the most basic human traits and experiences, the elements necessary for changing your life, achieving fulfillment. Through these books, you too can join others, who are seeking the very same things as you. The benefits of The Seven Laws of Nature are far-reaching and eternal. No better books are available. They supersede all others.

Dr. Gayle F. Arrowood

Riverside Community College

Praise for...The Seven Laws of Nature By Dr. Mushtaq H. Jaafri

"... I found 'The Seven Laws of Nature,' very intriguing. I too am a firm believer in synchronically and coincidences." – Betsy Gallagher, Freelance Writer, Ontario, CANADA

"... After going through The Seven Laws of Nature, I was very impressed with the writings. I found it dificult to put down. I found Dr. Mushtaq Jaafri to be a true role model and inspiration to a lot of people" – Keith R. spanarelli, Training specialist, LA Times

"... What makes this book a must read one is that Dr. Mushtaq Jaafri shares his philosophy, concepts, and real-life experience with you." Ron Schneider, Waco, Texas

"... For the short time I've known Dr. Mushtaq Jaafri, I can say he is a remarkable human being. He is doing the human family a great service through his writing. I would personally like to recommend The Seven Laws of Nature book."— Aman Ali Haj, Riverside, Calif.

"... I am happy that our paths have crossed. It's so wonderful to meet a 'like' believer. Thank you for the gift, The Seven Laws of Nature book."— Annie, Victorville, Calif.

"...I must admit this is one of the most amazing books I've read in a long time. I couldn't put it down. I just had to write you." – Ivan Zitek, Brompton, CANADA.

"...The benefits of The Seven Laws of Nature are far-reaching and eternal. No better books available. They supersede all others." – Dr. Gayle F. Arrowood, Hemet, Calif

"...I am amazed at your work. What I've studied so far is perfect.Will be interested to hear more about your organization of spiritual people." – Dr. C.E. Littin, Keys, California.

My Personal Guarantee

When you finish reading and studying this book, I personally guarantee that your knowledge of your true-Self will be much greater than when you started. However, your mind is not a computer and can't record everything for instant recall.

Like most professionals, you will occasionally need reference books to find answers. That's why you'll want to keep this book, along with your other good books. I encourage you to read other self-help, motivational books. If you have any comments about this book or suggestions for its improvement, please let me know.

I wish you well in your search to find some answers about what makes this life tick. May God Bless You - always – and IN ALL WAYS. Amen!

Purpose

I want to help men and women discover the laws of their own nature and learn how these unseen dynamic forces make or break them. The Laws of Human Nature are the root of everything that happens to them, good or bad…success, riches, friendship, happiness…or disaster.

Man or woman never breaks a law of nature…he or she breaks himself or herself! The Laws of Nature are the laws of life, and are nature's way to live. Knowing these laws assure us of the highest and best way to enjoy life.

The last laws man would learn are the laws of his own nature, said Goethe.

Philosophy and psychology for everyday living, these basic Laws of Human Nature reveal the principles that determine the quality of each life and give the answer to the most important questions of life "Who am I?," "What my existence really means?" Be prepared, when you begin to put this philosophy of *The seven Laws of Nature* into action, for a changed life which will not only ease the trials and stresses of living, but will also prepare you for the accumulation of material riches in abundance.

Introduction

You are about to become acquainted with a power 'secret' that may change your entire life style completely, just as it has mine. But, before you and I become involved in this intricate and unique way to transform your life, let's have a heart-to-heart talk. I'll talk and you'll listen, okay

A few years ago, through my own stupidity and an offer for a business venture in the Middle-East, I lost everything that was precious to me: my home, my belongings, and my business. Down on my luck and no place to go to, I began to wander around, searching for myself and some answers that would make life bearable.

I spent much time in local parks and in public libraries because these were free and warm. Hoping to find a royal road to riches and fortunes, I joined several secret fraternal organizations. Day by day, I began to sink deeper and deeper into depression. Totally broke: financially, emotionally, and spiritually, out of desperation, I made some drastic changes.

And the way I made these was to stop feeling sorry for myself and blaming others for all my misfortune. I decided to totally commit myself to discovering the 'secret' of all human achievements by reading as many books as I could find. My passion, my mission, my obsession had become to find out what was the one 'key' secret of all successful people in all walks of life. I wanted to know the difference between me and all the people who were successful. I wanted to know the one foundation key to all human success both in personal as well as professional life.

So, I began the search…

I read as many books as I could possibly find (750+ to be exact) on human development, personal motivation, and self-help. I also read books on the Science of Mind and in Metaphysical Science, I read books on all religions. I spent year-after-year, reading (25+years to be exact), studying and understanding the one common denominator or the one foundation 'key' secret to all human achievements.

But, still the great 'secret' to all human achievements kept just a jump ahead of me. It was amazing that the ultimate power 'secret' was mentioned no fewer than a hundred or perhaps a thousand times throughout each great book I read, but nevertheless it did take me over twenty five years of constant searching and digging to uncover the suggestions and clues each author was giving me.

One of the main reasons it took me so long to uncover this ultimate 'secret' of all human achievements was that it had not been directly named, for it seemed to work more successfully when it was merely unfolded and left in sight where those who were ready for it and searching for it, might pick it up. It seemed as though this 'secret' to all human achievements somehow revolved around Seven Laws. But what were they? I just could not pinpoint any one of them.

So you can imagine the distress, frustration and agony I was going through for twenty five years because I was unable to put all the parts of the 'secret' together. And then finally it happened.

In the fall of 1980 (after 25 years of studies) during an hour of my greatest distress, I found my greatest *asset* in the discovery and revelation of my "Other-Self" the "God-Self" by reading a new-age philosophy of achieving the best in life by utilizing The Seven Laws of Nature. Sure enough, I could understand The Seven Laws of Nature. Let me explain!

This particular new-age philosophy I read said that each human being on this planet Earth has not one but TWO DISTINCT PERSONALITIES within himself or herself. One we see when we stand in front of a mirror. This personality is known as the PERSONAL-SELF that usually brings us misery, sickness, poverty, unhappiness and all the BAD things of life we do not want or desire.

And then, the other is the one we NEVER see when we stand in front of the mirror but rather we '*assume*' or 'feel' this new personality inside of us. This is known as the "God-Self!"

This 'God-Self" brings us health, happiness, peace, and prosperity and *all* the other GOOD things of life we do want or desire. This is the "Self" that lets us recognize within ourselves a greater potential and to use it to enrich the quality of our daily lives. This is the "Self" that is infinitely creative, infinitely loving and totally balanced.

It is the 'Self' that when totally discovered fulfills consciousness.

To my amazement, I discovered that a few throughout history have become *saints* through this ultimate experience of their minds. But I feel this is not the aim or goal, but to live life more productively by greater participation in it is the aim or goal.

Since 1980, I have been giving free lectures and seminars in The Seven Laws Of Nature throughout the world in churches and other philosophical and metaphysical societies. Truly, if all the world understood The Seven Laws Of Nature and then lived-by-them, indeed *all* the problems of the world would be solved; and peace, love, harmony and prosperity would be the experience of all humans. When you finish reading and studying this book, I personally guarantee that your knowledge of your true self will be much greater than when you started. However, your mind is not a computer and you can't record everything for instant recall. Like most professionals, you will occasionally need reference books (preferably ebooks) to find answers. That's why you'll want to keep this (ebook) along with your other good books. I encourage you to read other ebooks on self-help and motivation. If you have any comments about this ebook or any suggestions for its improvement, please let me know. My P.O. Box is 3698, San Dimas, CA 91773.

I wish you well in your search to find answers about what makes our lives tick. As a final word of preparation, before you begin the first chapter, may I offer one brief suggestion which will provide a clue by which the ultimate 'secret' may be recognized? It is this – *all of creation, everything that exists in the physical world, is the result of the manifestation of The Seven Laws of Nature, because these are the very same principles nature uses to create everything in material existence – everything we can see, hear, smell, taste or touch.*

The whole purpose of this unique ebook is to help each man and woman discover the laws of his or her own nature and learn how these unseen dynamic forces make or break him or her. The laws of human nature are the root cause of everything that happens to them, good or bad ... success or failure ... happiness or disaster. Man or woman never breaks a law of nature ... he or she makes or breaks himself or herself! The Laws Of Nature are Nature's Laws to Successful Living.

Knowing and obeying them *assure* us of the highest and best way to enjoy life.

Now let's go over The Seven Laws Of Nature and see how we can apply them in our own lives and learn to enjoy the best things life has to offer.

Chapter 1
The Law Of Universal Balance!

The first law of nature, The Law Of Universal Balance, is based on the fact that nature uses this universal law to keep a perfect harmony among other planets. It is this Law that provides the power or energy, which gravitates all bodies toward the center of the Earth.

Through this Law, a perfect system of *balance* exists among all stars, all planets, all matter, the sun, the moon, night, day, summer and winter throughout the universe. By this Law Of Nature, each is *fixed* with its own position and state and never interferes with others as they move through time and space.

Without this perfect universal balance, there would be constant chaos through collisions of stars and planets. Although this Law Of Universal Balance is primarily designed to control and run this universe, our creator has given each man or woman the privilege and the power to affect, use, and harmonize with the Law Of Universal Balance.

This is the very first 'secret' of all human achievements that I discovered, while applying The First Law of Nature. Somehow, every great human being on this planet earth, either consciously or unconsciously, understands this First Law of Nature and uses it to make life pay-off in terms of his or her choosing.

There is a beauty of *nature* all around us. It operates according to a perfect plan, which is a beauty. Look around you! Beauty exists everywhere. The affluence of the universe – the *lavish* display and the abundance of the universe – is an expression of the creative 'Mind of Nature'. The more tuned in you are to the Mind of Nature, the more you have *access* to its infinite, unbounded creativity. The point to remember is this: "there is an *energy* available in the universe, which you and I have the power to use it. What this simply means is that being a human you and I have been given the power and the privilege to use this very *same* universal Law which controls and runs the universe to control our own destiny here on earth. This is the first 'secret' that *you* need to know about this law.

To fully understand just *how* our universe operates according to a perfect plan, you must first recognize, relate, assimilate and apply (known as the R2A2 principle) this Law of Universal Balance to your own life on a daily basis.

In a psychic nut-shell then, The First Law of Nature says that there is an *energy* available in the universe and every man or woman has been given the power and the privilege to harness it to shape his or her destiny here on earth.

This *energy,* not only controls and runs the universe according to a perfect plan, but also allows the two personalities within us to work together as partners. Once you fully understand this mental phenomenon, you then begin to realize that your true-Self (the one you do not *see* when you stand in front of a mirror but, rather *assume* or 'feel' within yourself) is one of pure potentiality.

By realizing this fact, you then automatically align your personal-self with the *energy* that manifests everything in the universe. Suddenly, you begin to see through your physical body to your own true spirituality. When you discover your true-Self (and know who you really are), that knowing itself has the ability to fulfill any dream you may have. It draws people to you, and it also draws things to you that you want and desire. It magnetizes people, situations, and also circumstances to support your own dreams. (This is also called the support from the Law of Universal Balance.) This basic law of man and woman's nature revels the principles that determine the quality of each man or woman's life and give the answers to the most important questions of life. When you finish reading this entire book, you will know a lot more about yourself and about successful living, which is the highest art and science; very few learn the ultimate secret.

Every man and woman has two Creators … his or her God … and himself or herself. The first Creator furnished the raw materials and other gifts; the second Creator is what *we* make of ourselves. Each individual builds his or her own monument, or digs his or her own pit. Your life will be no better than the plans you make and the action you take.

You are the architect and builder of your own life, fortune, and destiny. You'll have a clear insight into your own personality, if you apply the Nature's Laws to successful living.

Two Things You Should Know!

I want you to know about yourself. If you understand the following two things and take them to heart, your own life will *never* be the same. I guarantee it.

First, *you* have a very special and unique talent to give to others. How do I know this? Call it a hunch. Now – please understand I'm not saying this to praise you or to glorify you in any way, shape or form (unless it happens to be true in your own case). I remember I had a very hard time accepting this truth: everyone has a special and unique talent to give to others. I kept on saying to myself, "Yeah – Sure, I have a talent." I almost threw the book out of the window, and I will tell you why? Because; I was just an immigrant from Pakistan, (I'm now an American citizen), who couldn't speak much English, and had a very hard time getting admission to some of the reputable colleges and universities in the United States of America. So you can imagine I was pretty skeptical about what I was reading in this book. But, then, I also knew that skepticism, in connection with all *new* ideas, is a characteristic of all human beings. And when I did follow the First Law, my skepticism was soon replaced by belief; this soon solidified into an absolute faith.

Very few people perceive the importance of the natural Laws. Even though the Laws of Human Nature are abstract, they are still a fact. One of the biggest proofs of the validity of this power of The First Law of Nature came by writing this book (now in its 3rd edition) to share with you as an ebook on the Internet. Only the Internet has the capability to reach millions of readers instantly worldwide. It will not surprise me one bit, if that power of the universe, which gave me the wisdom and the special and unique talent to write it, will also make this a national Best Seller on the Internet. I've seen it happen more than once.

Please understand, I don't say all this to impress you. I tell you all because it impresses me! Just think of it. If a person like me with no special talent and with all these language handicaps can learn Nature's Laws to Successful Living, so can you. I guarantee it.

So – the very first thing I want you to know about yourself is that *you* too have a special and unique talent to give to others. In fact, yours is special, so unique that only you can do it better than anyone else in the whole world. Ponder on this for a moment.

Just think of it! "You have a talent, so unique there is no one else *alive* on Earth who has the very same talent, or the ability to express that talent. Furthermore; there is a unique *need* for your special talent When this need is matched with the creative expression of your talent, you will ignite the spark in the Mind of Nature which will help you access its infinite, unbounded creativity. Expressing your special and unique talent to fulfill your needs could very well create an unlimited wealth and abundance for life. This is the monumental 'key' of all human achievements. Knowing that *you* too have a special and unique talent to give to others, and there is no else alive who can do it better than you. Every adversity you have faced in the course of your life-time, no matter how unpleasant, no matter how unfair, was in reality a step forward toward your own aim or goal in life. In no other way, could you have been brought to this point in your life. You now know about your own inherent God-given special and unique talent.

Previously you may have had a logical excuse for not having forced life to come through with whatever was asked, but that alibi is now obsolete because you are in possession of the 'key' that unlocks the door to life's bountiful riches. The 'key' is intangible, but powerful: the privilege of creating *in your own mind* a burning desire to share your special and unique talent with others. There is no penalty for the use of the 'key', but there is a price you must pay if you do not use it. The price is failure. There is a reward of stupendous proportions if you put the 'key' to use. It is the satisfaction that comes to all who *conquer self and force life to pay whatever is asked.* The reward is worthy of your effort. Will you make the start and be convinced? All you have to do is to capitalize on your own inherent God-given special and unique talent. That's all.

What is the second thing I want you to know about yourself, you may Ask? Just read on and you'll know very shortly. I guarantee it!

The second thing and a very important one I want you to know about yourself is that you too have a very definite major goal or purpose in your own life – and when you blend your special and unique talent with service to humanity, you will experience your own true-Self, the God-Self within you. As you have guessed, that whole idea behind the understanding of The First Law of Nature is to allow your two personalities (physical and spiritual) to work in a perfect harmony as partners. When you achieve this, you'll have gained access to the infinite, unbounded creativity by being in tunes with the Mind of Nature. Soon you will discover your *mission* in life for which only *you* were chosen to fulfill.

Now I know that it is very heavy stuff to digest, but believe me when I tell say its true. You do have a special and unique talent, and it's so unique that only you can it best. Remember there is a very definite need for your special and unique talent. Sharing it with others is why you were created. This is your purpose, your goal or aim and mission in life.

Think about this a moment!

Your own mission in life, and only you were chosen to fulfill it because there is no one else alive on Earth that has the same talent, or able to express the talent. Furthermore, let me tell you your mission mainly deals with service to humanity – t o serve other fellow human beings. It is of utmost importance that you know this vital fact about the nature of your mission in life. Fulfilling this mission could very well create an unlimited wealth and abundance for a lifetime.

Now – here's the bottom line!

You'll have to find your purpose and mission in life on your own, then find ways and means to fulfill it. How do you do that? Well, the whole purpose of this unique ebook is to help people like you and I, worldwide, to find their mission in their life and fulfill it. it took me more than twenty five years to find mine which is *to help you find yours.* All I ask is that you have an open mind. That's All. If you too happened to be skeptical like me, believe me I understand. But, at least, I was willing to apply the first law of nature as though my life depended on it (and it did at that time). Soon I began to gain material possessions beyond my wildest dreams. I found my unique and special talent by sharing the Laws of Nature by writing about them, and I found my mission in life by learning and living these Laws of Nature and by helping others to find their mission in life and help them fulfill it.

It took me twenty-five years to find my real purpose and mission in life which is to help *you* find yours. Do not be skeptical like me and waste much of your remaining precious life as I did. All I ask is that you have an open mind as you walk with me through the pages of this unique, one-of-a-kind ebook. You may accept or reject the information. The vital decision rests with you. In 1984, The Seven Laws of Nature philosophy became a part on my doctoral degree theses at the University of Metaphysics in Los Angeles, California. I've been giving lectures and seminars for the last twenty five years.

One of the most commonly asked questions is, *"How can we apply the Law of Universal Balance to our lives?"* My answers have always been this: "If you want to enjoy the benefits of the Law of Universal Balance, or if you want to make full use of the creativity which is inherent in the Law of Universal Balance, then you have to have access to it." One way to access it is through understanding of just how this First Law of Nature called The Universal Balance operates according to a perfect plan in our solar system where Earth and nine other planets are constantly revolving around the Sun.

As they travel, a perfect system of *balance* exists among them, never interfering with other planets, as they perform their duties while *fixed* permanently in a position until their intended time. Ponder on this perfect system of universal balance because herein lies the 'secret' of applying the Law of Universal Balance in our own lives.

Let me explain!

"In our Solar System, Earth and Nine other planets are constantly traveling around the Sun." So what? You say. Well … Likewise, in our Mental System, all kinds of thoughts *and* emotions (both negative and positive) are also constantly traveling around our Minds.

The point I'm trying to make is simply this: we can compare the Solar System of the universe with the Mental System of the human Mind. Now, much like the planets that occupy a certain *fixed* position in the Solar System, in the very same way *all negative thoughts and emotions occupy one fixed position in the mind, while all positive thoughts and emotions occupy another fixed position in our Mental System.*

At the risk of oversimplifying the concept of both the Solar System and the Mental System, let me say that in our Solar System, these planets never interfere with each other because of the Law of Universal Balance; in the very same way, our negative and our positive thoughts and emotions will *never* interfere with each other in our Mental System.

The 'key' to remember is two fold:

(1) Thoughts and emotions, both negative and positive, good and bad, happy and unhappy, constructive and destructive, are *constantly* traveling around the Mind.
(2) These thoughts and emotions (whether negative or positive is immaterial) *never* interfere with each other. One of the profound truths about our own Mind is the fact that *no two thoughts or emotions can occupy the human mind at the same time.* This is the 'secret' that allows you to apply the Law of Universal Balance in your life.

So – since only one thought or emotion must occupy the mind at any given time *and* since it will not interfere with any other thoughts or emotions in the mind, we can deliberately keep our own mind *fixed* 'on' the circumstances of life we do desire and want – and – completely ignore all other circumstances of life we do not desire or want.

Can it be done? Yes! Very definitely. How? "Through a strictest self-discipline. This is the one foundation 'key' I discovered to the proper use of the Law of Universal Balance.

UNDERSTAND AND ADAPT TO THIS TRUTH, OR PERISH, IS THE WARNING.

You see, through your self-discipline, you may *think* yourself into or out of any circumstances of life. Self-discipline will help you to control your own mental attitude. Your mental attitude is your most priceless possession and may help you to master every conceivable circumstance of life, and it will eventually introduce you to your Other-Self, the God-Self, the 'Self' you do not see when you stand in front of a mirror. Your mental attitude will allow your two personalities to work in harmony as partners. Your mental attitude will enable you to harness the *energy* available in the universe. When it appears, you'll recognize it. Whether you receive the sign in the first or the last chapter, stop for a moment when it presents itself and turn down a glass, for that moment will mark the most turning-point of your life. Remember too as you go through this unique ebook, it deals with universal facts and not fiction, its purpose being to convey a great universal truth through which all who are ready may learn *what* to do and *how* to do it! But, perhaps the biggest reward of the recognition of the *energy* available in the universe will come in knowing that this intangible power will convert every adversity, every defeat, every failure into an asset of equivalent scope. You'll eventually be able to recognize that the very same power which controls and runs this universe is also at your disposal for your own good. You'll learn to accept each and every moment *"As Is"* and NOT as it should be. You'll know that it is so because the whole universe is "*As Is"* and *you* too are an integral part in the scheme of this universe.

If you keep at it, a very wonderful thing is going to happen to you. Your dominating thoughts and emotions will send out psychic *energy* and they are united on a psychic-level with all other minds on Earth who are also operating on the same energy level, and thus will guide you toward the right people, the right opportunities just at the right time that will make all of your desires and wants a reality.

If you apply and then live by the First Law of Nature, you'll always be confident about your future, regardless of what is happening at the moment, *knowing* the very same power that controls and runs the universe is also working on your behalf to direct your life for good only.

You might wonder why if men or women have always had this power available to them, this fact has eluded the awareness of mankind in general for so many years. Part of the answer is self-knowledge has never been one of our strong points. To the contrary, even the most elemental knowledge of oneself is something that most people resist with the greatest determination. Usually it is only when we are in a state of great pain or confusion, and only self-knowledge offers a way out, Are we willing to risk our cherished ideas of what we are? And even then many people prefer to live a meaningless life rather than to go through the often disagreeable process of coming to know themselves.

In addition, there are some aspects of ourselves that are harder to know than others. For instant, the two distinct personalities within us. My twenty-five years of extensive research reveals that each one of us have not just an outer physical personality but also a spiritual personality inside of us. Each personality is an entity by itself. This concept is as real as any function of the human body, but somehow rejected for so long. I believe it's time for this truth to be told.

The power of the Law of Universal Balance has been acknowledge since the beginning of recorded history. However, the simplicity of the law has frequently been overlooked. That is why most people shy away even from attempting to apply this powerful yet simple and highly effective life-changing law.

I've been personally applying it to my own life for the last twenty-five years. I can honestly tell you it really does work, if you work at it. I have personally used it to pull myself out of many tailspins during the last twenty-five years. During this time, I have used this power to overcome many, many financial crises as well as personal and emotional problems.

The feeling that there is an *energy* available in the universe and you too can use it as something you never get tired of. The affluence of the universe – the lavish display and the abundance – is an expression of the creative Mind of Nature. I'm an integral part of that universal mind. The more *tuned-in* I am to the Mind of Nature, the more I have access to its infinite, unbounded creativity. You too will soon know what I am tell you is true.

But, first, you have to go beyond the *turbulence* of your inner mental dialogue to connect with that powerful, abundant, affluent, infinite and creative Mind of Nature. Once you do your part in controlling your thinking and emotions, then you too create the possibility to connect with power that controls and runs this universe. What better benefits can you ask for?

Finally, let me say this: "If you learn just one lesson only from the first law of nature, let it be this: from this day forward, you *accept* EACH AND EVERY MOMENT – "As Is" – and NOT as it should be. Just think about it for a moment! Once you begin to recognize the truth that each daily moment is "As Is" because the whole universe is "As Is," you then begin to let your personal-Self work in harmony with your true-Self, the God-Self. Once you do, you allow the very same power of the universe that controls and runs it to direct your own life for good only. Believe me when I tell you that there is no separation between you and this power of the universe. The more you experience yourself (Your Other-Self), the closer you are to that power of the universe. It draws people to you, and it also draws things you desire and want in life. You enjoy bonding with people, and people enjoy bonding with you – your power is one that comes only from knowing your own true-Self, the God-Self.

As you apply the Law of Universal Balance, this power will reveal itself to you.

I guarantee it.

Applying The Law Of Universal Balance!

I will put The Law of Universal Balance into effect by making a commitment to take the following steps:

(1) I will get in touch with The Law of Universal Balance by taking time each day to 'fix' my own MIND "ON" the things I

desire and want in life, and "OFF" the things I do not desire or want. This will introduce me to my Other-Self, the God-Self!

(2) I will take time each day to be more tuned-in to the Mind-of-Nature, and to have access to its infinite, unbounded and huge creativity and to silently witness the intelligence within every living thing. Spending time in nature will also give me access to the qualities inherent in The Law of Universal Balance.

(3) I will begin my day with the statement: "Today, I'm successful. The door before me is opens." Throughout this day as I go about my daily business, I will remind myself to accept each moment AS IS — and NOT AS IT SHOULD BE.

(4) I will take time each day to allow my TWO DISTINCT PERSONALITIES to work together in harmony as partners. My true-Self will reveal my own special and unique talent to share with others. I will sit silently whenever possible and watch a sunset, listen to the sound of running water, smell the scent of a flower, watch birds fly. But, mostly, I will witness the role of nature in my spiritual growth. In the ecstasy of my own silence, I will cherish and embrace those precious moments.

Chapter 2
The Law Of Harmony & Attraction!

The Second Law of Nature is called the Law of Harmony & Attraction, which is based on the fact that nature uses it to produce things after their own kind. The basis for this Second Law of Nature is that The Law of Harmony & Attraction simply translates everything into their own counter-parts.

Through this Law of Harmony & Attraction, a perfect system of Harmony & Attraction exists among all things in the universe. For example, a seed of an oak tree will produce an oak tree just as surely as the seed of a pine tree will produce another pine tree.

Through this Second Law of Nature, an animal will produce another animal, and human beings will produce after their own kind. The Second Law says the very same *energy* available in the universe, which converts an acorn into an oak tree and a caterpillar into a magnificent butterfly, causes water to flow through gravity, teaches birds to fly, fish to swim or flowers to blossom and is at your disposal to work on your behalf by the Law of Harmony & Attraction.

Although this Law is primarily designed to make the universe fruitful and multiply after their own kind, nevertheless our Creator has given us the privilege and the power to affect, use, and harmonize with this Second Law. This is the second 'secret' of all human achievements I discovered while applying the Second Law of Nature. There is a beauty of nature all around us. Look around you. Beauty exists everywhere. The affluence – the lavish display and abundance of the universe –is an expression of the creative Mind of Nature. The more tuned-in you are to the Mind of Nature, the more you will have access to its infinite, unbounded creativity.

There is no separation between you and this power. The more you experience your true-Self, the God-Self, the *closer* you are to that energy available in the universe.

The Seven Laws of Nature, in the form (ebook), which you now receive them, have come a long way from the first edition in a few small pamphlets. Today, it is greatly enlarged over the first edition and in a convenient text ebook.

It has risen to dominant importance in shaping not only my life, but has also led to actually changing the lives of more than a score of men and women whom I taught. In the beginning I gave free lectures and seminars in The Seven Laws of Nature philosophy. I would talk to anyone with a willing ear to listen.

I was amazed and delighted to discover that practically every individual I taught knew of these laws of nature, although some called them by other names, such as unseen forces, intangible power, super consciousness, and some even called the laws as a universal Mind.

As you see, they all virtually say the same thing: there is an *energy* available in the universe and you and I have the power to use it. I'm saying these laws really work, if you work them.

I must admit I've had my fair share of skeptics during my teaching career. But, I knew that skepticism, in connection with all new ideas, is characteristic of all human beings. I would tell them: if you practice these laws as revealed to you, your skepticism will soon be replaced by belief; and this, in turn, will soon become crystallized into absolute faith. One of the most frequently asked question was, "Is the second Law of Nature just an abstract One?

My answer: "Very few people perceive the *importance* of the Second Law of Nature. Even though it is abstract, it is still a fact. A Law by itself is a cold fact. It comes to life with human experience."

When we apply it, we allow the human experience to tie into the Higher-Power of God. We cannot define or explain any of the real values of life, such as love, beauty, truth, friendship, creation, God.

They are the most stable things in your life and yet you cannot define them. You can only experience them. We do not explain … we can only state, and this is all we can do with a large proportion of all the facts and truths we know.

Abstract truth or law can only be made to live as it is translated into human experience. No matter how true a statement about a Natural Law may be, it is only a skeleton until wrought upon the magic of human experience and made to live. Let The First and Second Law of Nature open your eyes to a better way of life. It is foolish to go against Nature's Laws to successful living; you'll become your own judge and hangman.

Use this knowledge to increase wisdom, so that you can have a better world in which to live. Always live an enlightened life, because you are here to grow. Live your life from God's view-point. Do not do anything unworthy, and you'll be blessed greater than your fondest dreams.

No man or woman will ever find a Law of Nature wrong. While everything around you is changing, these Laws are the most dependable source, which helps you to develop the greatness and goodness that lies within you. Here's nature's way to successful living, which is based upon the knowledge of, and obedience to, The Laws of Nature. You are about to start on the most beneficial quest ever into the knowledge, principles, and laws that govern this universe, including mankind.

Discover them and, therefore, the highest human enterprise ... the greatest wisdom...is the *only* path to the best life known. Ignorance of The Natural Laws is responsible for the misery of this world. Ignorance of them is also responsible for the seven major enemies of mankind namely: Fear, Hate, Jealousy, Superstition, Greed, Revenge and Anger.

To open the door, you must have a key. The Laws of Nature hold the key to successful living. The First and The Second Law of Nature will help you plan your way of life and live happily. Knowing and obeying these two Laws of Nature will make you as rugged as a mountain with a heart as tender as a child.

Obedience to them is the way mankind was designed to live. The rewards are many; contentment and inward joy will fill your soul. One important benefit is how your poise will be preserved at all times, asleep or awake; thus you'll retain the spiritual connection between your Spirit and the Spirit of God.

Suddenly love, peace and joy will flood your soul. The problems of the day and the struggles of your life will evaporate. Your sorrows will disappear through the understanding and use of nature's little secrets. The outside affairs of the world are all immaterial to you when you learn to live from within.

By the time you finish reading this ebook, you'll know a lot more about yourself and successful living. Such business is the highest art and science which you'll learn.

One of the most amazing things I learned during my 25+ years of personal research and studies was that the starting point of *all* achievement is desire. The finishing point is that brand of knowledge which leads to understanding – understanding of self, of others, The Laws of Nature, happiness. This sort of understanding comes in its fullest only through familiarity with, and the use of principles and The Laws of Nature as out-lined in this unique ebook.

To fully understand just *how* the Law of Harmony & Attraction works according to a perfect plan, you must first recognize, relate, assimilate and apply (R2A2) it to your own life on a daily basis.

In a psychic nut-shell then, the Second Laws of Nature says, "your negative thoughts and emotions will produce after their own kind; just as surely your positive thoughts and emotions will produce after their own kind.

This is the monumental 'key' behind the proper understanding of The Second Law of Harmony & Attraction. Part of the most important work, which anyone engaged professionally in the self-help field must do, is to explain the preceding to people – to make them understand that our Minds are like magnets, attracting back to them the nature of their dominating thoughts and emotions on a daily basis through The Law of Harmony & Attraction.

For example, when you allow your mind to fear poverty or lack or any other negative thoughts or emotions, and once they take hold of your mind, then The Law of Harmony & Attraction makes that a reality.

Why? Because, the mind is a very impartial thing. It will work on whatever *you* feed it, whether negative or positive. Your own mind has to produce the counter-parts of your dominating thoughts or emotions, which is The Second Law of Nature. So, it is your duty to safe-guard against any negative thoughts or emotions, making sure that only positive, creative thoughts or emotions dominate your mind, *at all times and at all costs.* This is the price that you must pay, if you want to be tuned-in to the Mind of Nature. It's true your life is what your dominating thoughts and emotions make it. In other words, you are what you think.

How can we apply this Law to our own lives? If you want to enjoy the benefits of it, or if you want to make full use of the creativity which is inherent in The Second Law of Nature, then you have to have access to it. One way to access it is through understanding the principle of just *how* "LIKE ATTRACT." Through this Second Law of Nature, all thoughts or emotions (whether negative or positive) will be translated into their own counter-parts.

In other words, thoughts of riches, abundance, happiness, wealth, peace and prosperity attract their own counter-parts, just as surely as the thoughts of poverty, lack, unhappiness, suffering, pain, disappointments, struggles, sorrows and frustrations will attract their own counter-parts.

Likewise thoughts (emotions) of Fear, Hate, Jealousy, Superstition, Greed, Revenge and Anger will attract their own counter-parts, just as surely as thoughts (emotions) of Desire, Faith, Love, Hope, Caring, Romance and Enthusiasm will produce their own counter-parts. The point to remember is that your own mind is like a magnet, attracting back to it the dominating thoughts or emotions through The Law of Harmony & Attraction.

Translated into daily living, a person, who is struggling financially should be taught that just by reversing his or her own thoughts (emotions) from negative to positive and from poverty to riches, will surely begin to attract to them individuals and /or opportunities or circumstances that will help them prosper.

A person, who is lonely and has a feeling of being unloved, should begin to *'think'* of themselves as person who is already loved, because they are a person who is capable of giving much love to another person.

The Second Law of Nature explains why most people go through life being unhappy and poor; their dominating thoughts and emotions are "ON" these circumstances of life. By the same token: when your dominating thoughts and emotions are "ON" the things you desire or want in life, and when you constantly 'feed' your own mind with positive, creative, universally inspired thoughts and emotions, then The Second Law of Nature takes over and make them a reality. You are already beginning to understand just how this Law can transform your whole life, bring you everything you have ever wanted or desired in life, and urge you to go forward.

Now – how does all this work as far as the daily living of a person? Well, my answer: People who think of their lives in terms of poverty or lack are operating consciously on this negative energy-vibration frequency;, hence, the chronic poverty thinker is attracted to other poverty thinkers as they are attracted to him or her.

Conversely, prosperity thinkers attract and are attracted by other prosperity thinkers who help the other upward in financial matters, while the poverty thinkers get together only to constantly complain how hard times are.

In a psychic nut-shell then, bad-time thinkers attract bad-times, and good-time thinkers attract good-times, through The Second Law of Harmony & Attraction.

Finally, let me say this:

If you learn just only one lesson from The Second Law of Nature, let it be this, when a person comes to himself or herself and discovers his or her true-Self, the revelation is usually due to a great sorrow or perhaps a failure in a business venture or to some physical affliction beyond his or her own control.

I'll say 'amen' to that, because due to my one and only great sorrow, due to the failure in the business venture in the Middle East, I discovered the *new* way to my soul, through this experience of the Inner-Most level of the mind.

The true-Self, the God-Self reveals itself through silence more readily than through the noises of our mad rush to accumulate material things beyond our needs.

This experience of the true-Self (our Other-Self) is available *only* to those who properly interpret and relate to this Second Law known as The Law of Harmony Attraction.

When you discover your true-Self, The God-Self and you know who you really are, in that *knowing* itself is the ability to experience your Inner-Most level of the mind. This experience alone can help you *assume* or feel the two personalities within you.

All those who have experienced it intuitive agree with me it is an experience where one has become one with the stars, nature, all living things and the universe. You will truly feel a universal oneness with all things, and you begin to appreciate the *energy* available in the universe. You will feel a bond with people and things as well as becoming more in-tune to the Mind of Nature. Spending time in nature also gives you access to the qualities inherent in The Law of Universal Balance. You silently witness the intelligence within every living thing. Silently sit and watch a sunset, or listen to the sound of running water, or simply smell the scent of a flower, watch a bird fly, fish to swim all in the ecstasy of your silence. This universal oneness within oneself may last only a few second when experienced as a mind expansion experience, but it's effect, even if experienced only once in a person's lifetime, remains the major influence or criteria "Identity-Structure" in the individual. Such is the power of The Second Law of Nature.

There is one thing that I want you to know about yourself. If you truly understand and take it to heart, you'll never be the same person again. I guarantee it.

"Only you have been given the power and the privilege to harness the very same Law that converts a tiny seed into a magnificent oak tree in order to shape your own destiny here on earth. Why? You may ask. Well – for one thing, just for having lived this life as a human being. What other reason do you need? Remember you are a very special person. You were created superior to all of God's other creations. You have been given a special and unique talent to give to others. In fact, this special and unique talent is so unique that only you can do it the best in the whole world. Just think of it! You have a talent that is so unique there is no one else alive on this planet Earth who has the same talent or the ability to express that talent. Furthermore there is a unique need for your own special talent, and when this need is matched with the creative expression of your unique talent, you will ignite the spark in the creative Mind of Nature.

Expressing your special and unique talent to fulfill your needs could very well create an unlimited wealth and abundance for you for life. You also have a mission or perhaps purpose in life, which deals with service to humanity –to serve your fellow human beings. When you blend your special and unique talent with service to others, you truly experience your Other-Self or the God-Self.

From this day forward, all you have to do is to apply The Second Law of Harmony & Attraction consistently. It will surely place you in a favored position with people, situations, circumstances or anything else you may need or desire. Every time.

Don't expect your own logical reasoning (no matter how sound it may appear to be at the moment) give you the answers. Expect your own intuitive mind to give you the answers. How? By applying The Laws of Nature on a daily basis. This is the price you must pay for everlasting happiness.

If this second Law is so powerful, then why have so few availed themselves of all the benefits of this universal Law. My answer: The simplicity of The Second Law of Nature has frequently caused it to be overlooked.

The more you experience yourself –Your True-Self – the closer you are to the power of the universe. This power draws people and things to you.

Like me, you too have to find your purpose in life and your mission on your own, then find ways and means to fulfill that purpose or mission. Otherwise your life will not be complete. I have found mine. And I don't mind sharing it. It is simply to help *YOU* find yours and then to fulfill it.

Now –go and apply The Law of Harmony & Attraction. We will reconnect again. Peace!

Applying The Law Of
Harmony & Attraction!

I will put The Law of Harmony and Attraction into effect by making a commitment to take the following steps:

(1) I will remember the very same power that converts an acorn into an oak tree and a caterpillar into a magnificent butterfly is at my disposal to work on my behalf by The Law of Harmony and Attraction. I will make sure only positive thoughts and emotions dominate my mind at all times and at all costs. I will not allow my mind to fear poverty or any other negative thought or emotion.

(2) I will access The Law of Harmony and Attraction through understanding the principle of just how "likes attract." I will know through The Second Law of Nature all thoughts (whether negative or positive) will be translated into their own counter-parts.

(3) I will remember when I discover my own true-Self and when I know who I really am, in that knowing itself is the ability to fulfill any desire I may have. I will not expect my logical reasoning (no matter how sound it may appear to be at the moment) give me the answers. I will expect my own intuitive mind to give me the answers.

(4) I will remind myself to practice "Present-moment" awareness in all my actions. I will accept the present moment "As-Is" and not "As-It-Should-Be." I will refuse to allow negative thoughts and emotions to consume and dissipate the quality of my attention in the present moment. I will affect, use, and harmonize with The Law of Harmony and Attraction by mentally accepting the fact that a law has to have a human experience.

Chapter 3
The Law Of Cosmic Habit Formation!

The Third Law of Nature is called the Law of Cosmic Habit Formation. This Law is based on the fact that nature forms a cosmic habit through *repetition*. The basis for This Third Law is that it simply produces a definite pattern to keep the *same* momentum by repeating it over and over again.

Through this Law a perfect system of momentum exists among all stars, all planets, all matter, the sun, the moon, night, day, summer and winter throughout the universe. By this Law of Nature, each is *set* in motion with its own position and never interferes with others as they move through time and space. Without this cosmic habit formation, there would be no time or space.

Let me explain!

Our Creator (God) created everything for the overall purpose of this universe. Sun was created to produce day, planets were created to revolve around the Sun, moon to follow night, summer with winter, water to flow down.

And then all of these creations were engineered and designed to *confine* to a cosmic habit through repetition. It was intended all these creations must follow that same, set cosmic habit. Through this Cosmic Habit Formation, the Sun was risen, and the Sun was set, night followed the day, all seasons of the year followed each other.

Then each one of these creations was set in a definite motion, and each remained so until they all produced a very definite pattern. This definite pattern was taken over by the Cosmic Habit Formation, which in turn produced the energy necessary to keep the momentum going until its intended time and space. Through this Third Law of Nature, a perfect system of balance and momentum exists in the universe where the Sun, Moon, Day, Night, Summer and Winter perform their chosen duties like a clock work.

Although this Law of Cosmic Habit Formation is primarily designed to keep the momentum going in the universe, our Creator has given each man and woman the privilege and the power to affect, use, and harmonize with the Law of Cosmic Habit Formation.

This is the third 'secret' of all human achievements that I discovered while applying The Third Law of Nature. There is a beauty of nature all around. Nature operates according to a perfect habit through repetition. Beauty exists everywhere. The affluence of the universe –the lavish display and abundance–the graceful movement of planets – workings of the universe –is an expression of the creative Mind of Nature.

The more tuned-in you are to the Mind of Nature, the more you have access to its infinite, unbounded wisdom and creativity. Remember "there is an *energy* available in the universe," you and I have been given the power and the privilege to use this very same energy, which keeps a perfect system of balance in the universe, translates everything into their own counter-parts, helps us be fruitful and multiply, and keeps a perfect system of momentum in the universe.

Just think of it!

You and I have the power and the privilege to use the very same energy that controls and runs it to shape our destiny here on earth. This is the third 'secret' you need to know. If you remember nothing else from this chapter, let it be: "Nature's Laws govern human nature. Your job is to discover and benefit from them; you are not concerned with man-made laws."

Nature's Laws and common sense, simple Laws are what our discussion is all about. These you shall learn, then live by and hopefully share with others whether it be your spouse, a child, a friend or a business associate. This knowledge will eventually alter culture here on Earth. The Natural Law is the inherent law of man and woman's nature, and its principles are known to all and obligatory on all.

The knowledge of Natural Laws are a product of human experience and reason. The wisdom it provides was gained by men and women of different faiths, of no faith and is reflected in human experience.

I'm always asked this question: "Are The Laws of Nature scientific laws?"

My answer: "The Laws of Nature are indeed, unseen, intangible forces; but as they work the same way over and over again, they can be called scientific laws which are as dynamic as any, or all, scientific laws. A bird lives in the air … its natural environment. A fish lives in water … its natural environment; in the very same way, mankind lives in laws … unseen, intangible forces pervade and govern the entire universe, including the nature of man or woman.

Human perception of beauty in nature is the very first step toward the *energy* available in the universe. Look around you. Beauty exists everywhere. Nature operates according to a perfect plan, which itself is a beauty. When you can appreciate beauty all around you and learn to simultaneously give it back, you'll have learned The Third Law of Nature.

In short, The First Three Laws of Nature, working in collaboration with each other, allow your two distinct personalities to work together in harmony as partners. When you realize your own true-Self (God-Self) and know who you really are, in that knowing alone is the ability fulfill any desire you have.

When you discover the true-Self is one of pure potentiality, you then align with the higher power that manifests everything in the universe. It draws people to you, and it draws things to you that you desire and want.

It magnetizes people, situations, and also circumstances to support your dreams and goals of life. Successful living is based upon the knowledge of This Third Law. (This is also called the support from The Law of Cosmic Habit Formation).

I often wonder why I was given the opportunity to discover The Seven Laws of Nature. I'm nobody. I used to ask this question: "Why Me? I am nobody." After years of pondering, I finally concluded "the universe did not care if I was nobody. All it cares about is that I learn and then *live* by these Seven Laws of Nature. That's all.

I became obsessed with this self-knowledge. I reasoned that since the whole purpose of life is to serve mankind, perhaps my own mission mainly deals with service to other fellow human beings by sharing this self-knowledge.

I said to myself, "Yes, I've got it. This is my mission in life. I just learn, then *live* by these Seven Laws of Nature, finally help others find and fulfill their own mission in life.

The idea of giving lectures and seminars was scary, to say the least. I had been an introvert all my life. I was always quiet in public, but somehow I knew this was my special and unique talent of which The First Law of Nature spoke.

The idea of writing a book was no more possible than walking on the moon, but here I am with five books already written on The Laws of Nature series. And I owe all this to the self-knowledge I gained by mastering The Seven Laws of Nature.

You may be wondering at this very moment: "why are there only Seven Laws of Nature?"

If you are, then my answer is that actually several hundreds of Laws govern and control this universe. Some Laws deal with the Mind; some, the Soul; some, Life itself. If you endeavored to master all the natural laws, it would probably take you a longer time than you have in one life time.

However, only Seven Laws concern us human beings. These Seven Laws are designed to open the door to your personal growth and fulfillment, the know-how for better living. Only these Laws give you the 'key' to a joyful and prosperous living and teach you the certain way to the only true, genuine and lasting success.

Ever noticed some people find and enjoy good experiences right *now*, while others keep hoping and waiting for the good things to happen tomorrow. Also, why is it some people live full, rich and happy lives, while others under equally favorable circumstances and with no less ability and opportunity, feel cheated and dissatisfied, as if life played a dirty trick on them. I found my answer in The Third Law of Nature. I discovered all these fortunate people, who live full, rich and happy lives and find and enjoy good experiences *now*, have somehow learned the art and science of connecting with the *energy* available in the universe, which of course is the energy of God. Your perception of beauty indicates how close you are to this universal *energy*. The reward is worth of your effort. Will you make the start and be convinced?

How can we apply The Law of Cosmic Habit Formation to our lives?

If you want to enjoy the benefits of The Law of Cosmic Habit Formation, or if you want the full use of the infinite, unbounded creativity which is inherent in this Third Law of Nature, then you have to have access to it. One way to do this is through the Law of Cosmic Habit Formation, understanding just *how* our own habits are formed.

In psychic nut-shell then our dominating thoughts and emotions, whether negative or positive, *repeated* over-and-over again, 'set' a very definite pattern in our mind. This pattern is taken over by The Third Law of Nature, and makes it a reality, by every means possible, through The Law of Cosmic Habit Formation.

The 'key' word here is '*repetition*' of the same thought or emotion, which sets a definite pattern in the mind to be taken over by The Third Law. Anything you *repeat* in your mind, either consciously or unconsciously, will eventually produce a definite pattern in your mind, which in turn produces the mental ENERGY necessary to keep the momentum and become a habit for The Third Law to take over.

Very simply stated then a loving thought or emotion produces one type of mental 'energy' or frequency or pattern, while a hateful thought or emotion produces another type of mental 'energy' or frequency or pattern.

Likewise a poverty thought is of one frequency, while a prosperous thought is of another. No matter what kind of a thought or emotion it may be, if it is *repeated* over-and-over Again, it will eventually set a definite pattern in your mind and will become a habit. Why? Because it's The Third Law of Nature at work.

And when you least expect, this *pattern* will be taken over by The Law of Cosmic Habit Formation and will make it a reality sooner than you think. This is a two-edged knife. Use it constructively, and it will make your dreams come true. Use it destructively, and it will kill you (so to speak) every time. Much like electricity, you can it use to serve you or kill you. The choice is entirely yours.

By realizing these known facts about the power of *repetition*, we can apply this third Law of Nature in our own lives through our choices. We can simply decide once and for all to 'choose' the only kind of thoughts we want to associate with, *repeat* them often until they produce a definite pattern and are taken over by The Third law of Nature, and has become a *new* habit. What will be accomplished with this new habit?

Herein lies the hidden 'secret' of your future great accomplishments. As you *repeat* your positive, creative, universally inspired words to yourself over-and-over again, they'll soon become a part of your conscious mind, but more importantly they will eventually 'seep' into the inner-most level of your mind, a mysterious source which never sleeps, creates your dreams, and often makes you ACT in a way you do not comprehend.

This *new* habit will let you experience the new YOU – and will let you 'assume' or 'feel' your true-Self, the God-Self. It will allow you to see through your physical body to your true spiritual individuality, your Other-Self, the one you don't normally see when you stand in front of a mirror. Recognize it. Appropriate it. This is the reason you were created to live this life as a human being. Your job is to let your two distinct personalities work together in harmony as partners.

One of the mediums for influencing the inner-most level of the mind is known as 'auto-Suggestion,' simply a term which applies to all suggestions (by yourself or others) which reach your mind. Stated in another way, auto-suggestion is self-suggestion, a suggestion to yourself, by yourself. Nature has so built man and woman that he or she has absolute control over the material (thoughts, emotions) which reaches the inner-most level of the mind.

Our dominating thoughts (Good or bad, negative or positive, constructive or destructive, happy or sad, healthy or sick) *repeated* over-and-over again 'set' a definite pattern in the mind, which will be taken over by the energy created by the pattern and transmitted to the Mind of Nature.

Through these Laws of Nature, our mind reaches the very same '*energy*' that keeps a perfect system of balance in the universe (first law), helps things to be fruitful and multiply (second law), and keeps planets in motion (third law), and helps us make our own desires a reality.

Just think of it! You and I have been given the power and the privilege to access the very same *energy* available in the universe which teaches a bird to fly, fish to swim, flower to blossom, converts a seed into an oak tree, a caterpillar into a magnificent butterfly, causes water to flow down, we can USE it to mold our destiny here on earth.

I hope that you don't take the power at your disposal lightly, because every man and every woman has two Creators (first God and second himself or herself). The first Creator furnished the raw materials (life, gifts); the second is what we make of ourselves by using this power. In short, life is a gift from God, and what we make of life is a gift back to God.

The most effective way to apply this third Law of Cosmic Habit Formation is through what is commonly known in the self-help fields as the "Auto-Suggestion" principle, simply repeating something to yourself over-and-over again.

When you repeat something to yourself (whether consciously or unconsciously), over-and-over again, you are applying the principle of self-suggestion or auto-suggestion.

The 'key' to remember is that at present the auto-suggestion principle is the one and only method available to activate the switch (so to speak) of your own mind that will produce the necessary pattern, which The Law of Cosmic Habit Formation will accept, recognize, and take over. Auto-suggestion is the only means (without any external stimuli) of influencing the sub-conscious mind. Auto-suggestion is the only path to reaching the inner-audience of your mind, to make your each and every desire and goal a reality.

You may have noticed I've repeated myself over and over again throughout each chapter in order to impress upon your mind the *key* words, phrases, sentences and eve phrases paragraphs, I would like for you to remember.

The more often you read, the more you understand; the more you understand, the more you'll actually use. Why? Because repetition is the mother of skills. By my self-suggestions and by reading the ideas, the messages over-and-over again, everything will soon begin to click and make sense. I guarantee.

Now – how does all this work as far as the daily living is concerned?

Well, much like the Sun, Moon, Summer, Winter, Day, and Night are all engineered and designed to *conform* to the very same daily routine or pattern through The Law of Cosmic Habit Formation, in the very same way our own dominating thoughts (whether negative or positive) repeated over-and-over again to ourselves by ourselves also produce a very definite PATTERN in our minds, through this Third Law of Nature.

It is in taken over by the *same* natural laws that convert an acorn into an oak tree, and keeps a perfect system of balance among all stars, planets, causes water to flow down, birds to fly, fish to swim and grass to grow in order to help us also to convert our own dominating, positive, creative and universally inspired thoughts and emotions into their own counter-parts.

In human relationships, this *energy* that runs and controls this universe (through the natural laws) will also convert every adversity, every defeat, every failure into an 'asset' of equivalent scope. But perhaps the biggest pay-off and benefit will come by protecting your own most priceless possession namely: *"Attitude"— from being negative to positive or from becoming destructive to constructive.*

Your mental attitude is the one and only thing over which you have full and complete control. You have no control over what other people say, do or think, but you have full and complete control over what goes into your own mind. Very simply stated then, The Third Law of nature goes something like this:

"Whatever a person thinks on the conscious level of the mind enters into the second level of the mind called the "Personal Sub-Conscious" or the memory-bank of the mind. Here, over a period of time, 'thought-accumulation' builds ... a thought-accumulation of both positive (winning) and negative (failure) thoughts in your mind. It is estimated that nine-tenth of a person's conscious reaction to events in daily living, from the most major occurrences to the most trivial ones are bases upon what a person has come-to-expect as a result of a computer-like feedback to the conscious mind from the "Personal Sub-Conscious" memory-bank of the mind.

The 'secret' to the proper understanding of this Third Law of Nature lies in the profound fact that whatever you *think* of every minute of every day (24 hours a day) goes into the second level of the mind, where over a period of time, a 'thought-accumulation' builds, one of both positive (winning) and negative (failure) thoughts in your mind. It in turn sets-up a definite PATTERN in the conscious mind, and is picked up by that power, the Law of Cosmic Habit Formation (which of course is the Third Law).

Here we are laying the foundation for the presentation of the fact of great importance to the person who does not understand why some people appear to be lucky, while others of equal or greater ability, training, experience and brain capacity, seem destined to ride with misfortune.

This fact may be explained by the statement that every human being has the ability to completely influence and control his or her mind. Nature has endowed us with absolute control over what we think, our thinking patterns. Every human being in this world has been given the power to fully and completely control his or her own mind. The only way you completely control your own mind is by simply controlling your thinking. And with this control, obviously, every person may *open* his or her mind to the tramp thought-impulses, which are being released by the other mind – or – *close* the doors tightly and admit only thought-impulses of his or her choice. Here your own self-control or self-discipline will come to your rescue. This fact – coupled with the additional fact that by controlling your own thinking, you control your own mind – leads us very near to the principle by which you can produce a very definite PATTERN that is easily recognizable by the greater (power) of the universe.

Remember this:

You may control your own mind. You have the power to 'feed' whatever thought, emotion, feeling you choose. Choose to 'feed' only positive thoughts, emotions or feelings, and do that at all times and all costs.

By applying The Third Law of Nature, you are actually engaged in trying to help 'shut-off' the flow of negative impulses or thoughts – and to aid in voluntarily influencing your sub-conscious mind through positive impulses of desires, aims or goals in your life by producing a definite PATTERN in your mind that can be taken over by The Law of Cosmic Habit Formation.

You either control your own mind, or it controls you. There is no half way compromise. As a human being, you control nothing in the sphere of life except your own thinking. This prerogative of being able to control your thinking gives you the full and complete control over your mind, and almost all other circumstances, which affect your life. Before we begin together the study of The Fourth Law of Nature – may I offer one brief suggestion, which may provide the 'clue' by which a '*Miracle' may be recognized.* The 'clue' is simply this: By giving us the control over our thinking, our Creator (GOD) intended us to have a priceless 'asset' because our own thinking is the one and only means by which we may plan lives and live it as we choose. Our Creator (GOD) gave us the complete r*ight* to control our thinking. Along with this profound *right*, we gain the reward for our exercising the positive, and terrible penalties for failure to do so.

Here then is the "Miracle!"

"Our privilege to take full and complete possession of our minds simply by keeping it so busily engaged in thinking of our desires, aims or goals in life that (literally) no time is left for us to think of anything else."

Verily, this "miracle" is so powerful that those, who eventually discover it, will receive with it the means of recognizing and bringing into service that power mentioned in the previously in Three Laws of Nature. Truly, that power now lies dormant, awaiting your recognition and call to service. It serves only those who call. But let me be perfectly honest with you and tell you that this is ONLY one half of the PASSWORD of that "Miracle." The other half must be added to this half in for the miracle to work. In the next chapter, the other half of the PASSWORD will be revealed to you. And hopefully you will recognize it, immediately appropriate it, and begin to transmute it into a full life of your own making.

The Fourth Law of Nature begins on the following pages of this ebook, but every word written before them is for the purpose of showing you the key to Successful Living and Well-being. When you finish reading this ebook, you will know a lot more about yourself than when you started. The business of proper living is the highest art and science. So I hope you'll discover this ultimate 'secret.'

Peace!

Applying The Law Of
Cosmic Habit Formation!

I will put The Law of Cosmic Habit Formation into effect by making a commitment to take the following steps:

(1) I will remember that one way to access The Law of Cosmic Habit Formation is by understanding just how my HABITS ARE FORMED. My dominating thoughts, whether negative or positive, repeated over-and-over again, will 'set' a very definite pattern in your mind, which is taken over by the Mind-of-Nature.

(2) I will choose the kind of thoughts I want to associate with and repeat them often, until they produce a definite pattern and are taken over by The Law of Cosmic Habit Formation. Through this third law of nature, my mind will reach the 'same' *energy* available in the universe that runs and controls it.

(3) I will witness the 'Choices' I make in each moment. I will try to make the 'Choice' of controlling my own mind by simply controlling my own thinking. And, in the mere witnessing of these 'Choices', I will bring them to my conscious awareness.

(4) I will know the best way to prepare myself for ANY moment in the future is to fully control my present thinking. I know it is my God-given right: the privilege to take full and complete possession of my mind. By giving us the control over our thinking, the Creator God intended this to be a priceless asset. Our mind is the one and only means by which we may plan our lives and live it as we may choose. This is a 'miracle' which our Creator gave us for having lived this life as a human being.

Chapter 4
The Law Of Compensation!

The Fourth Law of Nature is called the Law Of Compensation. It is based on the fact that nature uses this Law to promote a habit of giving before receiving. The basis for this Fourth Law is that it allows nature to reward individuals in exact proportion to their own just efforts.

But nature demands we put forth our own individual efforts first, *before* we can expect or demand to receive any rewards. In other words, we must do our part first in any undertaking and then The Fourth Law of Nature will do the rest for us.

For example, a farmer digs the land, fertilizes it, sows the desired seeds (whether it be rice, grain, wheat or fruit), and waters this ground or field for months and months without any sure fire guarantees of ever receiving any crops.

Once the farmer digs the land, plants the necessary seeds, waters it for months and does his job of whatever has to be done, then of course The Law of Compensation takes over. When the farmer has done his part first, he is usually rewarded a hundred or perhaps a thousand fold for each and every seed he sowed in the field without ever expecting any direct or immediate return. Nature demands we perform our just duties first. Why? Because it's The Fourth Law Of Compensation.

But when we do our just part first, without expecting an immediate or direct reward or compensation right away, then of course we are bountifully rewarded. One of the main weaknesses of mankind is the average man and woman's familiarity with the word "impossible." He and she know all the things which cannot work. This ebook is especially written for those who seek the laws which have made others successful and are willing to *stake everything* on those laws.

This ebook is written for those who would be willing to learn through the application of The Fourth Law of Nature,

COMPENSATION, the blessed art of 'giving' and the science of 'receiving'. They would definitely find wealth and affluence or anything else they may want or need in life.

In a psychic nut-shell then, the more you give, the more you receive, because you'll 'keep' the abundance of the universe flowing and circulating in your life. It's what you give to others which multiplies, and whatever you keep to yourself eventually diminishes.

In fact anything, which is of any value in life, ONLY multiplies when given. If it does not multiply through giving, it is neither worth 'giving' nor worth 'receiving'. If, through the 'act' of giving, you feel you have lost something, then that gift is not truly given and will not cause increase. Because this is the second half of the PASSWORD of the miracle mentioned in the previous law, which is capable of making you free – truly free.

I earnestly believe that a part of the most important work of anyone, engaged professionally in the personal self-development field, is to explain the preceding miracle to people –making them understand the art of giving and the science of receiving through the application of The Law of Compensation.

The lack of proper understanding of these four Laws of Nature is probably the root cause of failure in our present educational system in the United States of America and particularly throughout the free world. Please allow me to explain.

"Why is our present educational system failing?"

Many of us seem to think that just by teaching human beings to read or write, we shall solve our human problems. While it is obviously necessary to know how to read or write, it will not give anyone the capacity to understand life.

The ability to understand ourselves is both the beginning and end of all Education, which is not merely acquiring knowledge, gathering and correlating of facts, it is to see the significance of life as a whole.

This understanding comes only through ***self-knowledge***, which is an awareness of one's total spiritual process. Thus, education, in the true sense, is an understanding of oneself, for it is within each one of us that the whole existence is gathered.

What we now call education is a matter of accumulating information and knowledge from books, which anyone can do who can read. Such knowledge offers a subtle form of escape from ourselves. Like all other escapes, it inevitably creates misery.

Conflicts and confusion results from wrong relationships with people, things, nature and the whole universe of which we as humans are an integral part. And until we understand that relation, and more importantly alter it, merely learning, gathering facts and acquiring various skills, can only lead us to engulf chaos and destruction. The highest function of education is to bring about an integrated individual, who is capable of dealing with life as a whole person. Education, as it is at present, in no way encourages the understanding of the inherited tendencies and environmental influences, which condition the mind and heart to accept Nature's Laws to Successful Living.

The Seven Laws of Nature philosophy helps us to break through the negative conditioning and bring about an integrated human being. Any form of education that concerns itself with a part, and ***not*** with the whole of a man or woman, inevitably leads to increasing conflict and human suffering. *This is the wrong kind of education.*

The right kind means the awakening of intelligence, the fostering of an integrated life, and such education can create a new culture and peaceful world.

But in order to bring about this new kind of education, we must take a fresh new look at the spiritual side of ourselves. The Seven Laws of Nature hold the truth about human life, and the complete understanding of ourselves, which is an awareness of one's total spiritual process.

I earnestly believe, from the bottom of my heart, The Seven Laws of Nature should be taught in all schools, colleges, and universities. I also believe they should be a part of any curriculum of the Social Science, Human Resources or the Philosophy department at all major colleges and universities in the United States of America and the free world.

Not because they help you to cope with all problems of life, but more importantly, the whole purpose of education is, or at least so it should be, to start the mind of an individual to grow from within.

Truly, if all the world understood The Seven Laws of Nature and then lived by them, indeed all the problems would be solved; and peace, love, harmony, and prosperity would be the experience of all human kind.

I predict if The Seven Laws of Nature were properly taught in all schools, colleges and Universities, they would so revolutionize the entire educational system in the world that the time spent in schools, colleges and universities or in any other educational institutions would be reduced to less than half. I guarantee it.

Conventional education in the United States of America or throughout the free world, as it is at present, makes independent thinking extremely difficult. To bring right education into our homes, schools, colleges, universities or in any other educational institutions, we must obviously understand the true meaning of life as a whole. And for that, we have to be able to think directly and to truly and seek answers from within.

In a nut-shell then, ***The Seven Laws philosophy*** explains the whole physical world operates solely by an *energy* available in the universe, according to these Seven Natural Laws. This *energy* is the very same energy that causes the water to flow down, teaches birds to fly, fish to swim, changes an acorn into an oak tree, day into night, summer into winter and a caterpillar into a magnificent butterfly and millions of other tasks simultaneously without any effort or demand by anyone or anything.

The point to remember is this:

"There is a greater power in the universe; you and I have been given the power and the privilege by our Creator (GOD) to affect, use, and harmonize with it. We have the privilege to use this *energy* to change or improve the quality of our lives here on earth."

This *energy,* available in the universe, responds to human expectations, which create everything that happens to us in the physical world. If one can learn to connect and build up energy, then *coincidental events* can begin to happen consistently.

But you have to watch each *coincidental event* closely to discover what exactly is the message which is always contained in each.

How to connect and build up enough energy does not involve one law; it's all of them. Through these Laws of Nature, our mind reaches the very same 'energy' that keeps a perfect system of balance in the universe (First Law), and helps everything living to be fruitful and multiply (Second Law), and helps attract good luck in life (Third Law), and rewards our just deeds a hundred fold (Fourth Law).

The final three Laws of Nature deal with the personality-structure of every human being on earth. These laws provide all of the answers to all of the intangible needs for your mind, body and soul.

Each law provides a part of the whole, which you put together to help you learn to connect and build up enough energy, so coincidental events could happen consistently. But you have to watch each coincidental event closely to uncover the message in each one. By learning the full details of what each means, and how they work, we can construct a whole new view of life, *law by law*.

This will indeed be an education at its best!

It will convert every defeat, every failure, every disappointment into an asset of an equivalent benefit. In human relations, you'll learn human violence comes from our urge to control another human being. You'll know what happens inside a human being that makes him or her try to control someone else. We just do what makes us feel the strongest. All we know is that we feel weak, and when we control others, we feel better. But we don't realize this temporary sense of feeling better usually costs the other person. Yet once humans understand their sorrow and struggle, we will immediately begin to transcend this human conflict. We will begin to break free from the competition over mere 'human-energy', because we will finally be able to receive the 'universal energy' – a new source which will eventually stop all human conflicts. The Seven Laws of Nature philosophy deals with this human conflict issue.

It also deals with Nature's Laws to Successful Living, which will ultimately prepare you to attract and enjoy life right now, instead of waiting for things to happen tomorrow. As you apply these natural laws on a daily basis, one of the most important thing to remember is, *'that the problem in life isn't usually in receiving answers, but it's often in identifying your current questions'*. This is the monumental key to this philosophy.

So – what are your current questions? Identify them; then watch closely for the coincidental events to happen in your life. (You must follow this sequence). First, identify your current questions. Second, watch closely for the coincidental events to happen.

Why? Because the whole universe is *energy,* which responds to every human expectations. When you have a question, people or things or circumstances will show up with the answers, if you are ready.

During this third millennium, human culture will change dramatically as a result of our conscious evolution. Guided by these Seven Laws, everyone will know precisely what to do and when to do it. This will fit harmoniously with the acts of others. No one will consume *energy* excessively, because they will let go of the need to control others and will possess material things more than they need for security. Just imagine what kind of a place this world be in which to live.

Wouldn't you agree that this ***self-knowledge*** (not just the book-knowledge) is the true essence of all education. Is it any wonder why our present educational system is failing? (These are my own opinions. Any different view-points are welcomed.)

How can we apply the Law of Compensation to our daily lives?

If you want to enjoy the benefits of The Law of Compensation or if you want to make full use of the creativity, which is inherent in The Law of Compensation, then you have to have access to it. One way to do this is to access an understanding of the principle of "Going the Extra Mile" in everything you do, whether your personal, professional or social field, or something in human relationships.

Through this Fourth Law of Nature, all individuals will be rewarded for their just efforts, but nature demands we 'give' or render a useful service, *before* expecting to 'get' something in return.

In its simplest form – this Fourth Law of Nature works something like this:

"People in sales, for example, can utilize this Fourth Law by making specific numbers of calls daily, making full and complete presentations of their product or service, being focused in the field, keeping a positive mental attitude no matter what, and putting forth their diligent efforts to sell *and* close FIRST, before expecting any rewards, and always going the 'extra-mile' by giving more service than expected or by making more sale calls than expected or working longer than expected."

Once a sales professional does his or her just part, then his or her effort will be rewarded a hundred or perhaps a thousand fold. Why? Because it's the law. Just as a single 'seed' of grain, rice, wheat, or corn is sowed in the field and diligently served for months, it will surely produce a hundred fold in return for a farmer. In the very same way, a single sales call will surely produce a hundred fold in return for a salesperson. The only thing is we don't know *which* one of his or her single sales-calls will produce that hundred fold result.

This is the monumental 'key' behind the proper understanding of The Law of Compensation.

Knowing one single sales-call out of all the calls he or she made in the field will produce a hundred fold result – which one will produce that result, we don't know; but if he or she makes enough presentations daily with the right mental attitude, The Fourth Law of Nature will come to the rescue just as surely as there will be a tomorrow. A salesperson may have a bad day in the field, or he or she may even have an occasional bad week, but he or she will *never* have a bad month, once he or she has put forth the just effort first.

A salesperson, who *truly* understands the Law of Compensation, is the one you'll usually find attending all the prestigious company paid conventions and parties throughout the world. How do I know all this, you may ask? Well – I should know, because I too was in sales for more than twenty years. I personally have sold everything from office products to businesses to selling insurance door-to-door.

At times when I would make perhaps 25 to 30 presentations daily and not make a single sale. I knew my product and knew my rebuttals, but I just couldn't close any sales. But I knew selling is a numbers game; the law of numbers works if you work it. Someone ***will*** say "Yes," if you give enough presentations first. (It's called the support from The Law of Compensation).

But, I'll tell you what?

I won many prestigious President's Club awards during my sales career. I went to many company full paid trips to Las Vegas, Mexico, Utah. My recent trip was a 7-days fully paid trip to El San Juan Resort in the beautiful city of Puerto Rico.

A President's Club usually consists of a Company's most prestigious group of ones who produce. The qualifications of each year's President's Club are competitive; their outstanding efforts place them in an elite category, and they are always highly pleased with the luxurious tropical setting that awaits them. I've truly enjoyed these trips; it was like vacationing around the world with my wife and letting the company pay for the trips.

My office wall is loaded with all kinds of trophies and certificates of outstanding accomplishments and achievements in the sales profession. Was I the greatest salesman in the company? Did I know more about my product or service? I don't think so. Was I the most intelligent person in the company? I assure you I certainly wasn't? In fact, because of my heavy accent in the English language, many people had a hard time understanding my presentation. Then, why is it I won the President's Club awards. My answer is that I knew. The Law of Compensation, which rewards individuals in exact proportion to the efforts they put in without expecting any return first. That's all.

Please understand I don't tell you all this to brag or to impress you. I tell you all this because I want to give you, in a simple language, some proof of the validity of the soundness of The Fourth Law of Nature called COMPENSATION.

What I'm trying to say is that the *intention* behind your own willingness to put forth the necessary efforts first in any undertaking is the most important thing to make your dreams or goals a reality.

The rewards are always there, but the rewards are always in direct proportion to the intensity behind your efforts. The more you put forth your own efforts first, in any undertaking, the more rewards you'll receive through The Law of Compensation. Can this Law of Compensation work in human relations? You bet. "How?"

When, for example, a habitual negative thinker of many years becomes an ardent positive thinker—or the chronic poverty thinker becomes a prosperity thinker-we say it is indeed a momentous 'Change' in the personality-structure of the individual. This new 'Change' is the COMPENSATION for the individual's efforts to have a mind that operates effectively on the positive level of the mind. He or she learns to take the first initiative to treat all others as he or she would have themselves treated. They are the ones who realize that human conflicts begin with our desire to control others. They know human confusion results from our own wrong relationships with people, things, nature and the whole universe.

They realize that until we understand the relationship, and more importantly *alter* it, mere positive thinking alone, or being just a good guy, can often lead us to engulfing chaos and misunderstandings, and even in some cases to destruction.

I hope you understand by now that I'm only trying to introduce you to your "Other-Self," the "God-Self", who once it has been recognized will provide you with all the 'proof' you'll ever need or desire, which is only another way of saying that I am endeavoring to introduce you to 'look within' for all the answers to the riddles we call life. I don't mean to minimize the formidable problems still facing humanity, only to suggest each of us in our own way is involved in the solution to this riddle.

If we stay aware and acknowledge the great mystery of life, we will see we have been perfectly placed in exact the right position … to make all the difference in the world… One person-at-a-time. I've also seen The Law of Compensation work equally in the business world. I've noticed with profound interest just how people, who are quite astute in business matters, use this Fourth Law of Nature.

These smart business people utilize it by investing their own money first in products, in display advertising, Radio & Television advertising and other expensive promotions, and incentives and costly programs, knowing (either consciously or unconsciously), that The Law of Compensation will take care of their justly deeds and efforts.

And they, more often than not, are usually rewarded a hundred or perhaps a million fold for all their hard work and investments.

How does The Law of Compensation work in its highest form, You may ask?

Well – I'm now going to share an ultimate 'secret' to all human achievement in your personal, professional and social life. This is the *essence* of the Law of Compensation.

This little known 'secret' has literally changed my whole life.

I can earnestly say that what I'm about to reveal to you in only a few seconds might become the major influence or criteria of your own 'identify-structure' in your personality, just as it has mine.

IN ITS HIGHEST FORM –THIS FOURTH LAW OF NATURE-THE LAW OF COMPESATION WORKS SOMETHING LIKE THIS:

"The good we do for others 'sets' into motion the good in God's Mind, which returns to us many times over in the good we receive from others."

Please read and re-read this until you *know* its true. I still get a chill in my body and soul every time I read this. It has made me realize God is as much 'in-us' as God is 'all-about' us. It has taught me that anything of *any* value in life only multiplies when given. If you take this ultimate 'secret' to heart, your life will never be the same. I guarantee it.

It is said nothing in this whole universe is *static*. What I mean is Mind and Body and the whole universe are in a constant phase of what I call an "Exchange". That is why it is so important we MUST 'give' or render a useful service first, *before* we can expect to 'get' or receive.

In every adversity there are seeds of equal or more opportunities. In every seed there is a promise of thousands of forests. But the seed must not be 'hoarded'; it must be sowed, so that it can give its intelligence to the fertile ground. An adversity usually forces individuals to look within for the answers. It more often than not introduces us to our own special and unique talent and the purpose for which we might have been born. It explains our mission in life, which mainly deals with service to humanity. Truly, if all the world understood this Fourth Law of Nature and took full and complete possession of their own minds, and recognized their "Other-Self" (the 'Self' you don't see when you stand before a mirror), indeed all the problems of the world would be solved; peace, love, harmony and prosperity would be the experience of all human kind.

They will be in the flow of abundance of the universe by utilizing Nature's Laws to Successful Living. They will be the ones to be the world's first to eliminate the seven major negative emotions (Fear, Hate, Jealousy. Superstition, Greed, Revenge and Anger) from their minds for good and feed the positive seven major emotions (Desire, Faith, Love, Hope, Care, Romance and Enthusiasm) into their minds at all times.

Moreover; they would learn, through the application of The Fourth of Nature (called Compensation) the art of giving and the science of receiving, and they would definitely keep wealth circulating in their lives and in the lives of all others they meet. For this ***self-knowledge*** will surely give them the second PASSWORD for the miracle mentioned in the previous law, which is capable of making you free – truly free-from the bondage of all self-imposed limitations. I guarantee it.

Finally, let me say this: Unconsciously, I've been organizing this philosophy of personal self-development for the last twenty-five years, not knowing the research was intended for the birth of this ebook, the one you are now down-loading from your personal computer, or perhaps a computer of a friend or a loved one.

I spent about 20+ years investigating this particular philosophy of individual achievement by utilizing certain laws of nature. And then I spent nearly five or more years reviewing various literature on the lives and accomplishments of the greatest people this world has ever known as well as just the average people like you and I in all walks of life, who actually utilized these Nature' Laws to Successful Living in one form or another, either consciously or unconsciously.

The purpose of my five years review type research was to cross-reference the main themes in The Seven Laws of Nature with things I had researched to support these ideas. I was intrigued by the self-knowledge in The Seven Laws of Nature, to say the least. Most of the philosophical or Metaphysical studies I had done in the past were just too complicated to comprehend by an average person. Here, in plain language, were The Seven Natural Laws anyone with a little intelligence could easily understand. The object of my own research was to present to the world the unique contribution of my own ideas to the existing field of philosophy and metaphysics. My goal, my mission, my obsession became to present these Natural Laws, NOT as a standard text filled with pages of theory, but down to earth facts based on my personal experience. But, first I had to do *two* things to test the soundness of the validity of The Seven Laws of Nature.

Here are the two things:

First, I would submit my research in The Seven Laws of Nature philosophy as partial requirements for my Doctoral Degree thesis in the Science of Metaphysics at the University of Metaphysics in Los Angeles, California.

Second, I would spend twenty years or more preparing myself to take them to the world, to men and women, who without these laws might go through life as failures. I have kept my promise. This new, revised, (now in its 3rd edition) ebook, contains The Laws after having been put to a practical test by me and thousands of others who applied them.

So— what's the point for this long dissertation, you may Ask?

My answer: I spent over twenty-five years in research and studies in order to gather all the data base for the manuscript of this ebook.

Just think of it!

Twenty-five long years!

Twenty-five years of work without any direct financial compensation is an experience not calculated to give you sustained hope, I assure you. But I knew from the beginning that through the energy of the universe and the power of The Law of Compensation, I will be rewarded a hundred or perhaps a thousand fold for every *tiny* effort I have already put forth, when I do finally arrive.

In that, I've not been disappointment at all so far because it has enabled me to earn my Doctoral Degree in the Science of Metaphysics. Recently, I was mentioned in the Who's Who in Metaphysics, which is a most prestigious professional publication in the field of self-help and metaphysics. I was founder of an International Mind-Conditioning Society, an organization devoted exclusively to working principles of the human mind in general and the teaching of self-knowledge in particular. This is a worldwide society based in California. It will not surprise me one bit if the power of the universe, which gave me the wisdom to write this ebook, also makes this one of the world's Best Seller ebooks. It could happen, because I've seen it happen more than once.

The reason I know it could happen is that my major goal in life is to establish a scientific laboratory where people from all over the world come to 'connect' with each other and thus build a lasting bond, relationships and rapport. This is a place where people learn the full significance of the right education, then teach others, world-wide, the meaning of self-knowledge and the way it was meant to be taught in order to avoid failure in our society. I also believe this ebook may provide the missing link for reaching millions, worldwide, instantly for spreading this self-knowledge. How else can I explain the opportunity to work with 1st Book Library.

It is one of the leading organizations helping new authors get published on the Internet, which is comprised of many "sub-networks" that help organize various types of information. It is possible to target your information to any desired specific market, and since the Internet is connected with millions of computers linked together, you can instantly reach your specific market. Many experts agree that in our lifetime, the Information Superhighway (Internet or Net) will have a greater impact on our day-to-day living than anything else. By making this ebook available, perhaps my mission in life is about to come true through the power of The Law of Compensation. (It could happen.) Peace!

Applying The Law Of Compensation!

I will put The Law of Compensation into effect by making a commitment to take the following steps:

(1) I will always tell myself the good I do for others 'sets' into motion the good in GOD'S Mind, whereby the good returns to me many times from others. I will know that GOD IS AS MUCH "IN ME" AS GOD IS ALL ABOUT ME.

(2) I will remember that in every adversity there are 'seeds' of opportunity. In every 'seed' there is a promise of thousands of forests. But the 'seed' must ***not*** be hoarded; it must be sowed, so that it can give its intelligence to the fertile ground.

(3) I will make a commitment to myself to keep wealth *circulating* in my own life and the lives of all those I meet on a daily basis by giving. I'll practice the art of 'giving' and the science of 'receiving' I'll give the life's most precious gift: LOVE!

(4) Wherever I go and whoever I meet, I'll silently say … "I LOVE YOU!" This is a gift I can give to everyone I come into contact with, and this will start the process of circulating joy, wealth, affluence in my life and the lives of others.

(5) I will share this book with another person. I will help make this world a better place in which to live. I know anything of any value in life only multiplies when given. That which does not is neither worth giving nor worth receiving. If through the act of giving you feel you have lost something, then that gift is not truly giving and will not cause increase. Peace!

Chapter 5
The Law Of Eternal Sorrow!

The Fifth Law of Nature is called The Law of Eternal Sorrow. This Law is based on the fact that nature uses this law to communicate with everything in the universe. The basis of it is that through The Law of Eternal Sorrow, nature communicates with human beings, one of nature's clever devices by which we are kept from becoming enslaved by complacency and self-satisfaction. In its simplest form, The Law of eternal Sorrow works something like this:

"Nature forces us to take an introspective inventory of ourselves to search deeply into our hearts and into our souls for some answers to make life pay-off in terms of our own liking.

Sorrow, nature's clever device, forces individuals to look deeply for the seeds of opportunity in every adversity, every heart break, pain, suffering and disappointment.

Through sorrow, nature breaks up old habits and replaces them with new and often much better habits. Although sorrow is never invited by us, nevertheless it is one of the more effective devices of nature to condition our minds for success.

How can we apply The Law of Eternal Sorrow in our own lives?

If you want to enjoy the full benefits of The Law of Eternal Sorrow, or if you want to make full use of The law of Eternal Sorrow, then you have to have access to it. One way to access The Law of Eternal Sorrow is through the understanding of 'energy' and the bonding principle. In its highest form, The Law of Eternal Sorrow works something like this:

Everything in this universe is energy. The late Albert Einstein, world's greatest mathematician and scholar, proved this truth by his famous "theory-of-relativity."

He proved "ALL MATTER IN REALITY IS AN ENERGY – AND – ALL ENERGY IN REALITY IS A MATTER."

Very simply stated – "everything in this universe is connected with each other *through* energy, known as the nature's intelligence."

This also communicates with human beings through The Law of Eternal Sorrow, which is just one of nature's clever devices to keep us from becoming enslaved by complacency and self-satisfaction. It is also a clever barometer through which nature forces us to look deeply within for the answers.

Nature's intelligence functions effortlessly, frictionlessly, and spontaneously. When we are in harmony (Second Law) with nature, we as human beings communicate with this nature's intelligence or energy and ultimately by putting forth diligent efforts, we become one with everything (Fourth Law) as everything becomes one with us.

Now — how does all this work as far as the daily living of a person? Well, one sure fire way is to *think* of our own body (the one we see when we stand before a mirror) as a device for controlling energy. It is a well known fact that our physical body can generate, store, and expand all energy. If you know how to do these three things in an efficient way, then you too can create any amount of wealth, provided it does not violate the rights of others.

All you have to do is to learn how? When you are established in the knowledge of your true-Self, you too can make use of this nature's Intelligence. That's how.

Let's sum up:

The substance of the previous Four Laws is there is a greater power in this universe; you and I can use that power to mold our own destinies here on earth. This is the very same power that communicates energy to all living things. It gives life for the grass to grow (First Law), teaches fish to swim, birds to fly, flowers to blossom…

When we oppose nature's intelligence, we are actually opposing the entire universe. There is no separation between you and this nature's intelligence. The more you experience your own true-Self (God-Self), the closer you are to that power of the universe.

It draws people to you, and it also draws things that you desire or want in life to you. You enjoy bonding with people, and people enjoy bonding with you – your power is that bonding, one that comes only from knowing your own true-Self (the Other-Self).

The point I'm trying to make is that our habits, which do not conform to the over-all plan and purpose of this universe, are periodically broken up by this vital Fifth Law of Nature, The Law of Eternal Sorrow.

Nature leads man and woman through peaceful means as long as he or she cooperates, but nature resorts to revolutionary methods, if any man or woman rebels and neglects or refuses to conform to this Fifth Law of Nature.

After studying the case histories of several thousands of people and while putting this philosophy of personal self-development together, I discovered with profound interest that when a person comes to himself or herself and discovers that great power within his or her command, the revelation normally is due to a great sorrow or due to perhaps a failure of a business venture or due to some physical affliction *beyond* his or her own control. I'll say 'Amen' to that, because through my one and only great sorrow due to the failure of a business venture in the Middle East, I too discovered the new way to my own soul, which gave me my personal freedom. I would never have known it otherwise.

And it was this SORROW that actually led me through the chain of events toward the field of self-help, metaphysics and personal development, which gave me the opportunity to connect with you, build a lasting bond with other people throughout the world, and depart from this world as a more evolved soul. What more can anyone ask for?

Finally, I often thank my lucky star for having put me through this adversity. I would never exchange it for a billion dollars. If it was not for this adversity and sorrow, the manuscript of this ebook would never have been written.

It's true I had suffered both physical pain and mental anguish, but I had not quit fighting nor had I gone down under these circumstances. I had no financial means at that time, but I did have all the faculties of my own mind, and I intended to use those faculties as my Creator intended I should. I was created for a reason, and this sorrow had forced me to take an introspective inventory of myself to search deeply into my heart and soul for some answers to make my life pay-off in term of my liking.

I had lost my business, my home, and my belongings, but so had thousands of other men and Women. I was no better than they. Many of my friends and associates and relatives declined to give me a helping hand when I most needed it, but their refusal injured them more than it did me, for it had deprived them of an opportunity to be merciful to a helpless person & still left open a way by which I could regain my independence through the us of my mind. I do not regret the sorrow and the suffering I had gone through because it has given me the moral and mental stamina with which I shall gain for myself freedom in the future. And I don't hold any ill feelings against anyone for refusing to come to my rescue, because their neglect has provided me with a wonderful opportunity to comply with The Fifth Law of Nature, THE ETTERNAL SORROW.

During my sorrow and suffering, I had found the *seed* of an equivalent benefit. It consisted in my discovery of that power of my mind and the means by which it can be made to master sorrow and suffering.

This *seed* of an equivalent benefit also introduced me to my special and unique talent to give to others. It gave me new life, and a purpose for which to live. Just imagine, you probably wouldn't be reading this ebook, if it were not for the sorrow, the suffering, and the adversity I had gone through. Truly, in the hour of my greatest suffering and sorrow, I discovered my own soul, that invincible soul, the true-Self. I do not feel sorry for myself, but I do feel sorry for my own flesh and blood, because they were not ready to embrace a wonderful opportunity to discover the greatness of The Fifth Law of Nature. I also do feel sorry for all those refusing to come to my rescue, because they were not ready to embrace this once in a life chance to discover the greatness of their minds by exercising of mercy toward one who had the right to expect help from them.

This adversity, this suffering and sorrow has taught me a wonderful lesson: our true-Self (God-Self) reveals itself through silence more readily than through the noises of our mad rush to accumulate material things. I am also inclined to believe the God-Self and everlasting peace-of-mind is available only to those who properly interpret and fully relate themselves to this particular Fifth Law of Nature.

There are two things I want you to know about the essence of The Seven Laws of Nature philosophy. If you understand these two things and take them to heart, your life will never be the same. I guarantee it. Nothing will touch your life more than your ability to properly interpret and fully relate yourself to these two things.

First, *"the good you do for others 'sets' into motion the good in God's mind, which returns to YOU many times over in the good you receive from others".*

Second, *"Sorrow, suffering, and adversity (whether it be from physical pain or mental anguish), places one in a favorable position for an appeal to our Creator, God."*

In all fairness, let me say the pay-off never would have come, this ebook never would have been written and this philosophy of individual achievement never would have been organized had I not learned the blessed art of transmuting unpleasant circumstances into construction action.

REMEMBER ALWAYS THIS WORD: "TRANSMUTE"!

If you should ever feel your own sorrows are much greater than you can ever bear, then just keep your mind so busily engaged in thinking of something constructive that (literally) no time is left for you to feel any sorrow.

And if sorrow should overtake you, follow the same plan by turning your dominant thoughts towards the attainment of some as yet unattained purpose or goal and leave no time for self-pity, and then immediately devise means and plans and ways of attaining that aim or goal in life. DO THIS AND YOU SHALL SURELY DISCOVER A HIDDEN ASSET YOU DID NOT KNOW YOU POSSESSED.

You've got to go through the negatives to achieve the positive. The bigger the aim or purpose in life, the bigger is the sorrow, for this is The Fifth Law of Nature.

"The Secret-of-Secrets"

A few years ago, through my own stupidity and an offer for a business venture in the Middle-East, I lost EVERYTHING that was precious to me, my home, my belongings and my business. Down on my luck and no place to go to, I began to wander around searching for myself and some answers that would make my life bearable.

I spent much time in local parks and in public libraries because they were free and warm. Hoping to find the road to riches and fortunes, I joined secret fraternal organizations. I was totally broke: financially, emotionally, and spiritually.

Day by day, I began to find myself sinking deeper and deeper into depression. My own mind deteriorated rapidly. I lived in constant fear – fear that someone was chasing me, or fear that I was being killed. I remember walking in the night in a cold sweat, believing that I was falling, having jumped off a bridge. Another time, I thought that I was right in front of a bus which was about to crush my body.

These nightmares were so vivid I felt they were happening to me at that very moment. This went on night after night. It is a miracle I did not kill myself. One day, I had been walking all day, up until that evening. My body was aching as I lay on the bed. This time I felt that I was at the end of the road. I began to weep, and for the first time in my life, I got down on my knees and said over and over again, "God help me." "God help me."

Finally, I was able to sleep. As I lay there in that dark room, I began to dream. But this dream was different than ever before.

The next morning, I awoke suddenly with the dream still fresh in my mind. For a minute or two I stared at the bed room ceiling, remembering it fully. I had been making my way through a jungle searching for something. The jungle was large and exceptionally beautiful. In my quest I found myself in a number of situations in which I felt totally lost and bewildered, unable to decide how to proceed. Incredibly, at each moment of these moments, a person would appear out of nowhere as though by design to clarify where I needed to go next. I never became aware of the object of my search, but the dream had left me feeling incredibly upbeat and confident.

I sat up and noticed a beam of sunlight coming through the window across the room. It sparkled with suspended dust particles. I walked over and pulled back the curtains. The following night, just before going to bed, I got down on my knees again and said to myself over and over again, "God help me. God help me." Finally, I was able to sleep. As I lay there in that dark room, I began to dream again.

But, this dream was different from the night before. It was as if I was transported to the actual scene of the occurrence. As the dream began, I found myself on a darkened road at dusk. Night was setting in, but there was just enough light to make out the road ahead. As I peered down it into the distance, a bright light was shinning, so bright I couldn't look directly into it.

Somehow it was impressed upon my mind that at the center of this light lay the answer to all my problems. If I could reach this light, I would be given the 'Secret-of-Secrets'. My heart was pounding as I began to walk toward the light. Suddenly there loomed up in the path the figure of a man. I couldn't make him out in the darkness, but I could sense the evil as he stood brazenly blocking my path. Behind this creature appeared seven dwarfs.

Their eyes were shinning in the dark. I realized that the man and his seven helpers would do anything to keep me from traveling down the path toward the light.

A peculiar thing about this creature and his seven helpers was that each of the dwarfs wore a breastplate. On one was written the word 'Fear'. Others were labeled, 'Hate', 'Jealousy', 'Superstition', 'Greed', 'Revenge', and 'Anger'.

There was a breastplate on the larger creature too, but I just could not see well enough to make it out. I stood there trembling, wishing to move toward the light, but fearful of the dreadful creatures blocking my way. The larger one was snarling and making ready for battle. The seven behind him were snapping and clawing at the ground in their eagerness to devour me. Somehow, I gained a renewed will to survive and determined to go forward to the light. As I moved toward the larger creature, I was suddenly aware of the dreadful name written across the larger beast: 'Self'.

As I looked in the face of the larger creature, what I saw was a shock, almost too heavy to bear. It was my own face. "My God, how could that be," I wondered. The abhorrent creature I had so easily recognized in others was also within me.

I resisted, "Not Me," I shouted. I have always been generous throughout my entire life. I always insisted on picking up the tab. The drinks and the food were always on me. My home was always open to our friends. In fact, we entertained hundreds of close friends each and every week, giving free food, gifts and playing their favorite music and games. Suddenly, a deep voice came back from the distant light.

"Foolish man, with eyes that cannot see, you are totally selfish."

When have you lifted up a fellow *stranger* or comforted the *lonely*, the *old* or the *sick*?

When did you offer your coat or shoes to someone without one or reach out to touch the *needy* or place *bread* at the table of the hungry.

I awoke suddenly with a sweat and that dream still fresh in my mind. For a minute or two, I sat on the bed in the dark. As I sat there, I became vividly aware, for the first time in my life. I had never freely given anything that didn't hold the promise of reward or praise. It was the real me, the real Mushtaq Jaafri, face-to-face. I began to weep. Tears kept coming out of my eyes. I just couldn't stop.

As I asked God to forgive me for the selfishness that had dominated my entire life, I felt a new focus come into my life. Soon I drifted off to sleep again. The scene shifted back to the same narrow path with the bright light still in the distance.

I was brought back to the darkened path. As I proceeded fearlessly toward the larger creature and his seven helpers, my hand grasped at the one called 'Selfishness'. But I grasped only thin air. The larger creature suddenly vanished.

The dwarfs too had disappeared. Warmth came over me. "I *was* standing in the light."

For a swift moment, I was able to view the very heart of that bright light. Suddenly, there loomed up in the path of light a figure so radiant that only a glance was possible. Still I began to gaze at the light until I could make out what this figure was.

There was a word written across the light: "GOD!" Behind this figure appeared seven angels. Each of them also wore a breastplate: "Desire," "Faith," "Love," "Hope," "Caring," "Romance," and "Enthusiasm." I realized the brilliant light is merely a symbol for the existence of God, and the seven angels represented a pathway to reach God. Perhaps, for the very first time in my life, I truly understood that success could only be achieved through unselfish giving with no hope or longing for any reward.

Immediately, I understood pure love was beyond comprehension. God expects us to love – to help bring happiness into the lives of others. Suddenly, I knew nothing in life mattered more than love – love of God – and for one's fellow humankind. I realized that I had been chosen to witness this marvelous truth about human life to share it with the world.

Real happiness is possible only when we live our lives in harmony with our Creator God, who has certain laws that are universally true. As I lay in bed contemplating the truth, this self-knowledge, I began to realize if we do not conduct our lives within the framework of the God's laws, tragedy, disappointment and unhappiness will result.

I just sat there on the bed, staring into the emptiness, my mind captured by the dream that had just unfolded.

The scene replayed in my mind on a giant screen. Each night the light would flash, and I could see the shadow of the figure issuing from the source. I was able to view the very heart of light, so brilliant with radiance and power that only a glance was possible for a swift second. I had been living in darkness and was not aware of the creeping evil that had engulfed my life for so long. Since I stood in the light, I was now able to see my condition, and it was abhorrent. I could not wait to do something about it. It was urgent. I had gone through an inward cleansing and found I could tolerate the outward filth. That evening as I retired to bed, I set some goals I determined I would carry out during the next months. The next morning when I stepped out, I heard birds singing. I felt a warm stiff breeze on my face, which gently rocked the trees. The lake nearby was rippling and glistening this time of day, and I felt a chilly wind against my skin.

I touched a flower and wondered at the miracle. When had I noticed simple wonders? I was enjoying a peace that surpasses all understanding.

I said, "Good morning" to those who passed and they smiled and returned my greetings. Since I had been privileged to view the light, I would tell everyone I met I had been on a marvelous exciting journey. I told them I had discovered the 'Secret-of-Secrets'. You wouldn't believe the attention I received as I explained my dream.

I called old friends and customers, relaying my new-found experience to each of them. I travel a great deal. This business of sharing God's message has taken on an international flavor. I also give lectures and seminars on my experience.

In 1984, this experience became a part of my Doctoral Degree Theses under the title: The Seven Laws of Nature, written at the University of Metaphysics in Los Angeles, California. This experience has risen to dominant important in shaping, not only my life, but has led to actually changing the lives of more than a score of men and women whom I told the experience.

I pray my only motive in telling this story will remain – to touch the lives of all who listen, that they also might experience the satisfaction of living a less selfish life. I am deeply moved to know that many who have read my story have experienced dramatic changes in their lives, as they *adapted the principle of giving and love* People on the verge of a nervous breakdown have become whole again, simply by filling the void in their lives by developing concern for others. Problems vanish as they reach out to touch an orphan or attend some aged soul or visit an inmate in prison. Human conflicts diminish as an urge to control another human diminishes.

Families, torn by seven little dwarfs creatures namely: Fear, Hate, Jealousy, Superstition, Greed, Revenge and Anger, found the seven (heavenly) angels namely: Desire, Faith, Love, Hope, Caring, Romance and Enthusiasm. People who have heard my story have found renewed love and enjoyment in life as they took interest in each other.

To tell you about my personal giving and love would violate God's law of silence on this subject. I would like to say, however, that as I have reached out with my heart to help others, the resources to do so have come to me in a flood. All in all, I am at peace. I pray I will never be so busy I cannot take the time to search out those who are less fortunate than I and help them. This is, in the end, the 'Secret-of-Secrets' learning to give – learning to love. It is our fantasy, our heart's desire to be loved. Others want and need the same thing we do. For this is the 'Secret-of-Secrets' put in another way.

Final note:

I began to realize the whole purpose of life is serve mankind or humanity. When we choose actions that bring happiness and success to others, we achieve true greatness, success, and everything that comes with it. Human beings were put on this planet to 'connect' with each other and are the greatest resources we have. This bond, this rapport, will allow us to work together to produce results that we could never produce alone. We are now actively entering into what I call "The Information Age." During this new century 21st a major cultural transformation in using our mental powers will take place and will be the end result of people like you and I sharing this self-knowledge with each other. I predict, that within this new millennium, a universal bond or an international rapport will develop among the people of the world. If you are reading these lines, consider yourself lucky because you may be one of the chosen ones to spread this self-knowledge either locally through weekly home studies or perhaps worldwide by joining us. (More information is available from the author.)

The Laws of Nature will help you find your purpose or mission in life. It is your duty to find and fulfill it, mainly dealing with service to mankind. You were born for a purpose, not an accident. You were created for a reason. You owe it to yourself to find that purpose. The Seven Laws of Nature philosophy will help you find your purpose. I guarantee it.

In closing, the essence of The Fifth Law of Nature is this:

"You have got to get through the negatives go to the positives." The bigger your sorrow, suffering, pain or adversity, the bigger your aim or goal in life" For this is the essence of The Fifth Law of Nature.

Peace!

Applying The Law Of
Eternal Sorrow!

I will put The Law of Eternal Sorrow into effect by making a commitment to take the following steps:

(1) I will remind myself The Law of Eternal Sorrow is just one of nature's clever devices by which we release ourselves from being enslaved by complacency and self-satisfaction. Nature forces us to take an introspective inventory of ourselves, to search deeply into our hearts and into our souls for some answers that will make life pay-off in terms of our own liking.

(2) I will master The Law of Eternal Sorrow through the understanding of 'energy' and thebonding principle. I'll know all ***'Matter is Energy and Energy Matter'***. Nature's intelligence functions effortlessly, frictionlessly, spontaneously. When I am in harmony with nature, I attract the unbounded creativity of the universe and wealth to me.

(3) I will realize the most wonderful benefit I receive from my adversities consists in my discovery suffering (physical pain or mental anguish) PLACES ME IN A FAVORABLE POSITION FOR APPEAL TO MY CREATOR.

(4) I will understand the ultimate 'Secret-of-Secrets' is to 'give' – learning to love and to be loved. Others want and need the same thing we do. I will make a commitment to keep the wealth circulating in my own life and the lives of those I meet on a daily basis. I'll practice the art of giving and the science

of receiving. I'll silently say, "I LOVE YOU." This is a gift I can give to everyone I come into contact with, and it will start the process of circulating joy, wealth, peace.

Chapter 6
The Law Of Eternal Struggle!

The Sixth Law of Nature is called The Law of Eternal Struggle, which is based on the fact that nature uses this law to help humans become strong through resistance. The bases of this law allows *STRUGGLES*, in life, another of nature's clever devices to force all individuals to progress, expand and become strong through resistance. Through this Sixth Law of Nature, everything in this whole universe must go through struggles. Let me explain!

"Ever notice, the strongest trees are not those in heavily protected forests, but the ones which stand in open space where they are in constant *struggle* with wind and other elements of weather."

In the very same way, all individuals *must* experience struggles and undergo hardships in order to grow and become strong. Through this Sixth Law of Naturc, wc human beings accept all those so called struggles as mere circumstances of opportunities through which we may prepare ourselves for still greater and better planes of existence than the one on which we now dwell. It is said struggles are often a *test* from our Creator to see who will have the guts to get-up and make a fresh new start.

In doing my research and studies for putting this Sixth Law, I had noticed with profound interest no man or woman in the history of mankind was ever chosen as a leader, who had not been first thoroughly tested by The Sixth Law of Nature called The Law Of Eternal Struggle.

Problems become either a curse or a blessing for the individuals, depending upon just *how* it is taken. By utilizing this Sixth Law of Nature, we accept all struggles as a TRANSITIONAL stage leading to a greater good and abundance in our own lives.

How can we apply The Law of Eternal Struggle to our lives?

If you want to enjoy the benefits of The Law of Eternal Struggle, or if you want to make full use of the creativity which is inherent in The Law of Eternal Struggle, then you have to have access to it.

One way to access it is through the understanding the principle of 'self-preservation'. Let me explain.

Everything in this whole universe must go through struggles in order to progress and expand and become strong through resistance. Birds struggle to find food for themselves and for their offsprings.

They struggle to find shelters during rain, wind and all the other elements of weather. Flowers, plants and tree are in constant struggles in the forest to seek food and water. Weaker creatures are in constant struggles for survival from the stronger creatures. But such are not just limited to animals and human beings, they also break up old over-all plans of this universe, either by world wars, floods or earthquakes, epidemics of disease, and they force the universe to start all over again.

In its simplest form, The Law of Eternal Struggle works something like this: Through it, we accept all so-called struggles as mere circumstances of opportunities through which we may prepare ourselves for still greater and better planes of existence than the one on which we now dwell. After studying for the last twenty-five years, the case histories of countless thousands of people in all walks of life, I discovered no man or woman ever achieved riches, whether it be of material possessions or lasting inner-peace, who had not been thoroughly tested by The Law of Eternal Struggle.

Almost every person in this whole wide world, who achieved riches of either money or spirit in a big way, admitted that once he or she was so down in his or her personal, or professional or spiritual life there seemed to be no good reason to continue. They all admitted that the turning-point in their lives was this Law of Eternal Struggle.

Somehow it forces you to the point where everything is telling you to give up and quit trying. Some even go to the extreme, to the point of ending the life as a way out. It is usually at this point and at the peak of your depression when you usually begin to find the answers one-by-one to the riddle of life. I'll surely, say 'Amen' to that, because due to my one and only major struggle, the failure of the business in the Middle-East, I too was so down I even thought of ending life. I was literally forced to either end it or look for an opportunity to make a new start.

I was forced to struggle for twenty-five years to maintain myself economically, while doing the necessary research for organizing The Seven Laws of Nature philosophy in order to share it with the world.

The Law of Eternal Struggle revealed to me that in my adversity there is a 'seed' of an equal opportunity, which consisted of learning The Seven Laws of Nature, then living-by-them until they become my special and unique talent to give to others. I was given to understand that this special talent is so unique only I could do it best.

Just think of it!

"I had a talent so unique no one else alive on this planet Earth has the very same talent or the ability to do it. My self-esteem went to the roof, to say the least, when I discovered this vital truth about myself.

Furthermore, I was given to understand there is a unique need for my special talent. When this need is matched with the creative expression of my unique talent, I started to ignite the spark in the creative Mind of Nature, and thus helped me to access its infinite, unbounded creativity.

I began to ponder on the possibility of expressing my special and unique talent to fulfill my own financial needs, and I began to feel that with some luck it could ultimately create an unlimited wealth source for life. This became a 'mission', a purpose and an obsession and major goal in life for me. It has been a real driving force in my life. It has given me a reason to live. It has certainly propelled me toward my own spirituality and the metaphysical field.

I somehow felt this may be a 'mission' for which I was given the opportunity to live this life as a human being. I may have been chosen to share it with the world to serve mankind. After all, the whole purpose of life is to serve mankind or humanity. So I must fulfill it. I reasoned that when I blend my special and unique talent with service to others, I will experience my own true-Self, the Other-Self, the God-Self.

It has thus been nearly twenty-five years in my preparation to take this new philosophy, The Seven Laws of Nature. But you know I *can't* do it alone. It's a too big of a project. My hope is you'll find it in your heart and soul to give me a helping hand. I do need your support. (More about that later).

So, what's the point of all this? My answer: Twenty-five years of hard work, struggles and disappointments without any direct financial compensation is an experience not calculated to give one sustained hope, I assure you.

But this was the price I had to pay for the privilege of putting this new philosophy of self-development utilizing The Seven Laws of Nature. If this self-knowledge is able to transform your own life, no matter how small, or — if this self-knowledge becomes an integral part of the educational system in the United states of America or perhaps throughout the free world, then my twenty-five years of sorrow as well as struggles will have been well rewarded. And I do thank you and the educational system from the bottom of my heart. It would be as though I had finally arrived.

I must confess I have not been totally disappointed in my efforts, but I have been overwhelmed with the bountiful manner in which The Law of Eternal Struggle has responded and paid me tribute for the twenty-five years of sorrows and struggles that went into my work.

It was this struggle, which prepared me with the necessary self-knowledge that actually led me through the chain of events to my own 'mission' in life. This self-knowledge taught me I do have a special and unique talent, and I was to give to others, not just keep it for myself. Self-knowledge multiplies only when shared.

It was this self-knowledge that taught me that my talent is so unique that only I could do it best, and there is a definite need for my special and unique talent. What greater rewards can a person ask for. I found my own 'mission' in life by answering two most important questions.

(1) What do I want in life?
(2) Where Am I going?

Answer these two vital questions truthfully, so you too will have given your life a new purpose and direction. But more importantly, these two questions will surely lead you to your own 'mission' or purpose in life, just as it did mine and thousands of others, who took the time to answers these two questions.

The answers to these two questions will reveal some amazing things. So please do some soul searching or deep-probing while thinking about these two questions. They will surely pay you many dividends.

The answers to these questions will reveal, among other things, there is a definite need for your own special and unique talent. When you too match this need with the creative expression of your unique talent, you too will begin to access the infinite, unbounded creativity of the Mind of Nature.

Furthermore, expressing your special and unique talent could very well create unlimited financial abundance for life. All you have to do is to capitalize on your inherent, God-given talent. That's all.

When you blend your unique and special talent with service to others, you too will experience your own true-Self, the God-Self. I guarantee it.

Just remember this:

You too have 'mission' in your life for which only you were chosen to fulfill it. Your own mission mainly deals with service to humanity – and to serve your fellow human beings. The whole purpose of The Eternal Law of Struggle is to help you find your own 'mission' in life and fulfill it.

I'll ask you to go a step further: once you have found your own 'mission' in life, try to incorporate The Seven Laws of Nature by shifting the mind-set of your involvement in this material from the role of a mere learner to that of a teacher.

One of the best ways to learn anything is by teaching. Take your time, and read this material with the purpose in mind of sharing and discussing what you learn with someone else.

Read this material as though you are going to teach it to your spouse, child, close friend, business associate today or perhaps in a week while its still fresh in your mind.

Notice the difference in your mental and emotional process. You'll not only remember better what you read, but your perception will be expanded, your understanding deepened, and your motivation to apply it to your life increased.

As you openly and honestly share what you're learning with others, you will be pleasantly surprised to discovered any negative thinking or perceptions others may have of you tend to disappear. Those you teach will see you as a 'changing' growing person and will be more inclined to be helpful and supportive as you work together to integrate The Seven Laws of Nature philosophy.

A personal Invitation

As I conclude this amazing new ebook, The Seven Laws of Nature, I would like to share my own conviction concerning what I believe to be the main source of these Nature's Laws to Successful Living.

Correct principles are natural laws, and that God, the Creator of all human beings, is the real *source* of them and also the main source of all human conscience. To the degree human beings learn, then *live* by these Seven Natural Laws, they will grow to fulfill their own human nature; to the degree that they do not, they will not rise above the animal plane.

Parts of human nature *cannot* be reached by any other means except by the power of God. We cannot perfect ourselves. To the degree to which we align ourselves with correct principles, laws and divine endowments, we will be released to fulfill the measure of our creation.

I personally struggled with much of what I have shared with you in this unique new ebook. But the struggle was worthwhile and fulfilling. It gave meaning to my own life and enabled me to complete my own 'mission' or purpose for which I was born.

Almost anyone, who is seriously involved in any church activity regardless of the faith or denomination, will recognize churchgoing is *not* synonymous with personal spirituality.

Some people get so busy in church worship and church projects they become insensitive to the pressing human needs that surround them, contradicting the very precepts they profess to believe deeply.

There are others who attend church (mosque or temple) less frequently, or not all, but whose attitudes and behavior reflect a more genuine centering in the principles of the basic Judeo-Christian or Muslim or Hindu or other faiths.

Having personally participated throughout my own life in an organized Christian Church as well in a Muslin Mosque and community service groups in Los Angeles, California, I have found that attending church or mosque does not automatically mean living the principles taught in those meetings.

You can be active in a church (mosque or temple), but inactive in its gospel or preaching. In the church-centered life, image or appearance can become a person's dominant consideration, leading to hypocrisy that undermines personal security and intrinsic worth.

Because a church or a mosque or a temple is a formal organization made up of policies, programs, practices and people, it cannot by itself give you any deep, permanent security or sense of intrinsic worth.

Living the principles or laws taught by the church or a mosque or a temple can do this, but the organization alone cannot. Nor can a church, mosque, or temple give a person a constant sense of guidance. Church-centered people often tend to live, act, think and feel in certain ways on the Sabbath and in a totally different way on the weekdays. Such a lack of wholeness, unity or integrity is a way of seeing a church, mosque or temple as an end rather than a means to an end. It undermines a person's wisdom and sense of balance.

Although any religious organization claims to teach people about the real source of power, God the Creator of us all, it does not claim to be that power itself. It only claims to be one vehicle through which divine power can be channeled into man or woman's nature.

The Charter Ethic is based on the fundamental idea that there are principles that govern human effectiveness – natural laws in the 'human-dimension', which are just as real, just as unchanging and unarguable as are the laws, such as gravity in the 'physical-dimension'.

An idea of the reality – and the impact – of these principles or laws can be captured by Learning, then *living* these Seven Natural Laws. If you don't let the teacher know the level you are by asking a question or revealing your ignorance, you'll not learn or grow. You cannot pretend long, for you'll eventually be found out. Admission of ignorance is often the very first step in our education. Our growth requires our ignorance when we are using our knowledge.

The Seven Laws of Nature are not a set of separate or piecemeal psyche-up formulas. In harmony with the Natural Laws of human growth and development, they provide an incremental, sequential, highly integrated approach to the development of personal and interpersonal effectiveness.

They move us progressively on a Maturity-Continuum from our lower animal plane to rise above to the higher spiritual plane. My suggestion is that you try to master each Law step by step, because it is organized incrementally.

Also, try to shift the mind-set of your involvement in each Law from the role of a mere learner to that of a teacher. Take your time and read each law with the purpose in mind of sharing and discussing what you learn with one more person.

Read each law as though you are going to teach it to your spouse, child, close friend, business associate today or perhaps in a week or so while it is still fresh in your mind. Just remember that the best way to learn something is by teaching it to someone else. You should approach the information in each of the Law in this way; you'll not only remember better what you read, but your own perception will be expanded, your own understanding deepened, and your motivation to apply the laws increased. You'll notice the difference in your own mental and emotional processes.

As you openly and honestly share what you're learning with others, you'll be pleasantly surprised to discover any negative thinking or perceptions others may have of you disappear.

Those you personally teach will now see you as a changing, more evolved, spiritually growing person and will be more inclined to be understanding, supportive and helpful in any dealings you may have with them, as you work together to integrate The Seven Laws of Nature in their lives as well as in yours.

Just remember this: "The Seven Laws of Nature move you progressively on a Maturity-Continuum from a lower animal plane to rise above to the spiritual place of existence.

That's why Laws 1,2,3,4,5,6 in this unique new ebook deal with self-mastery. They move a person from dependence to independence. As you become truly independent, you have the foundation for effective interdependence.

The most effective way to begin is to develop a *personal mission statement* or philosophy or creed, which you'll live by. Your personal philosophy will focus on what you want to do (character). Your creed will focus on what you want to do (contributions and achievements). It focuses on the values, principles or Laws upon which your being and doing are based.

But, most importantly, search for your special and unique talent to share with the world. You too have a 'mission' or a purpose in life, which mainly deals with service to mankind or humanity. You must find and fulfill it. At the very least, you can share The Seven Laws of Nature with others. They will surely reveal your own mission to you, as they did mine and thousands of others who taught them to friends, relatives or associates. I was chosen by my Creator God to share The Seven Laws of Nature with others, in the hope that these laws will enrich their lives as they have mine.(You can read my whole story in the trade paperback edition of The Seven Laws of Nature Book).

I earnestly believe we are now in the process of actively entering into what I call "The Information Age," and during this new 21st century, a major cultural transformation in using mental powers will take place and will be the end result of people like you and I, sharing INFORMATION with each other. I predict within this new millennium, a universal bond or an international rapport will develop among the people of the world, and here's the reason.

Human beings were put on this planet to 'connect' with each other and are the greatest resources we have, This universal bond, this international rapport will eventually allow us to produce results together we could never produce alone. Because of this bond, and rapport, there will be a major cultural transformation that will be taking place in human society, and it will involve the use of our own 'Mind-Power', instead of the traditional 'Muscle-Power'.

This new cultural transformation in human society will be the result of work-a-day people like you and I, who are *not* necessarily religious in the traditional sense or churchgoing people, but very definitely spiritual people whose attitude and behavior reflect the very precepts of most, if not *all,* religions profess. The *core* of all this cultural transformation in human society will be the development of a universal bond or an international rapport among the people of the world. I've been chosen to receive The Seven Laws of Nature in order to form a core or a nucleus of a select group of work-a-day people and entrepreneurs, who will work together to build lasting relationships. By working *collectively*, we will change the 'thinking-habits' of the masses, worldwide, just as McDonald's changed the 'eating-habits' of the people around the world.

I'm now looking for people, who are not necessarily religious in the traditional sense, but very definitely spiritual people with values and who are blessed with 100% balanced personalities, or willing to become one by learning, then *living* The Seven Laws of Nature on a daily basis. (I call this the second phase of my mission).

Please don't misunderstand. "The knowledge of The Seven Laws of Nature isn't new. Individuals have been aware of these Seven Natural Laws throughout history, and this has been the perception behind many great attempts at philosophy and religion. But the difference now lies in the numbers. The cultural transformation in human society is occurring now because of the number of individuals having this awareness all at the same time, day or night, throughout the world.

The number of people, who are conscious of such Laws, would begin to grow dramatically in the middle of the twenty-first century. This growth would continue until some time near the end of the twenty-first century, when we would reach a specific number of such individuals—a level I think of as a critical mass. Once we reach this critical mass, the entire cultural will begin to take these Natural Laws seriously.

We will wonder, in mass, what mysterious process underlies human nature. And it will be this question, asked at the very same time by enough people, that will allow the other Laws to also come into consciousness, because when sufficient number of individuals seriously question what's going on in life, we will begin to find out that the answer exists in these Laws. Then the other Laws will be revealed … one after the other.

So, here's the 'key' to knowing when the culture will shift?

When enough people will grasp all The Seven Laws of Nature and begin to take these Laws seriously, culture will shift.

I was given to understand this was my 'mission' in life for which I was allowed the opportunity to live this life as a human being. You can read my full story in the trade paper back edition of The Seven Laws of Nature.

These Laws will show humanity HOW TO LIVE – BE – AND – HAVE THE BEST things life has to offer. Successful living is based upon the knowledge of and obedience to The Seven Laws of Nature.

Now that I've finally completed The Seven Laws of Nature in the form of an ebook, I seek a limited number of work-a-day people like you and I, who are not necessarily religious in the traditional sense, but very definitely spiritual, and whose attitudes and values and behavior reflect a more genuine centering in the direction of spirituality. This will be a once-in-a-lifetime opportunity for anyone interested in or currently engaged in the self-help or personal development field. If offers a chance to serve humanity by sharing this unique philosophy of individual achievement with others, while at the same time it will guide you toward your own special and unique talent. No experience necessary, we will train, but a positive mental attitude toward life in general and toward yourself in specific is a must. Desire to serve fellow human beings is a plus.

While none can predict the financial rewards of any new business venture, the rewards could be unlimited, because of our joint imaginations and our combined efforts to devise ways to share this self-knowledge with others.

The riches within our grasp cannot always be measured in money. There are great riches in lasting friendships, harmonious family relationships, sympathy and understanding between business associates, and inner harmony which brings peace of mind measurable only in spiritual values.

The philosophy of *The Seven Laws of Nature* will prepare you to attract and enjoy these higher mental states, which always have been and always will be denied to all except *those who are ready for them.*

Be prepared. When you begin to put the philosophy of *The Seven Laws of Nature* into action for a changed life, which will not only ease the trials and stresses of living, but will also prepare you for the accumulation of material riches in abundance.

Successful candidates are encouraged to learn these Laws and be willing to teach them either locally by 'groups-studies' or nationwide by joining The International Mind-Conditioning Society.

You may write to the author at his address. P.O. Box 3698, San Dimas, California 91773 USA. These select candidates will also act as one of the Board of Directors, and they will work together to guide the day-to-day operations of this California based non-profit organization called The International Mind-Conditioning Society, USA.

EVERYONE INVITED, NO FEES REQUIRED TO JOIN, IT'S FREE!

Applying The Law Of
Eternal Struggle!

I will put The Law of Eternal Struggle into use by making a commitment followings steps:

(1) I will accept all so called Struggles in my life as mere circumstances of opportunities through which I may prepare myself for still greater and better planes of existence than the

one on which I now dwell. Struggles are designed to help me grow through resistance.

(2) I will realize Struggle often becomes a curse or a blessing for me depending upon just how I take it. By utilizing The Law of Eternal Struggle, I will accept all those so called Struggles in my own life as a TRANSITIONAL stage leading to greater good and abundance in my life.

(3) I will realize the whole purpose of The Law of Eternal Struggle is help me find my own mission in life. I will ask myself daily: "What do I want in life?" "Where am I going?" "How can I serve other fellow human beings?" "What is my special and unique talent?" "What have I done in the past I can capitalize on to fulfill my needs?" "How can I have access to the unbounded creativity in Nature's Laws to Successful living?"

(4) I will talk about this book with everyone I will meet today. I know that the word-of-mouth advertising is the best way to pass on any good information. This is a book whose time has come to be passed from hand to hand, from friends to friends, a work that has come to light at a time when the world deeply needs to read its words. I will do my part to help connect with other human beings with similar interests, and thus build lasting bonds and relationships worldwide.

Chapter 7
The Law Of Eternal Change!

The Seventh Law of Nature is called The Law of Eternal Change, which is based on the fact that nature uses it to help human beings gain a capacity to adapt to *change* in order to progress. The basis for this Law is that so called *changes* in our lives is nature's clever 'tool' for human progress. Eternal Change is Natural Laws without which there would be no such thing as civilization.

Circumstances of life which change may just be a part of our Creator's over-all plan in connection with human destiny as a whole. It is said a change is often just a test from our Creator to see who will have the insight to accept a new direction in life.

The Law of Eternal Change and The of Eternal Struggle are known as two sides of the same coin, because they are Laws that nature uses to create everything in material existence — everything we see, hear, smell, taste and touch.

Through The Laws of Change and Struggle all individuals acquire flexibility of personality and the capacity to ADAPT themselves to all circumstances of life which affect them. Our *habits*, which do not conform to the over-all plan and purpose of this universe, are periodically broken-up, either by world wars, floods, earthquakes, epidemics of diseases, and we are forced to start all over again.

Nature leads human beings through Change or through Struggle by peaceful means as long as they cooperate, but nature resorts to revolutionary methods, if human beings rebel and neglect or refuse to conform to these Two Laws of Nature.

Remember this fact about these two tales or nature and profit by them the next time you happen to meet face-to-face with any Change or Struggle in your own life. Consider the possibility of a test from your Creator (GOD) to see if you have the insight to 'accept' a whole new direction in your own life.

And, instead of crying out in rebellion, or shivering with fear, hold your head high and look in all directions for the *seed* of an equivalent benefit in every circumstance of Change or Struggle.

How Can we apply The Law of Eternal Change in our own lives?

If you want to enjoy the benefits of The Law of Eternal Change, or if you want to make full use of it's unbounded creativity, then you have to have access to it.

One way to do so is through understanding just how to relinquish your attachment to material things. To acquire anything in this physical world, you have to *relinquish* your attachment to it first.

Relinquishing such attachment does not necessarily mean that you totally give-up your desire or the intention to create your desire. You don't give-up the intention, and you don't give-up your desire, *you only give-up your attachment to the result. That's all.*

The moment you relinquish your attachment to the result, you must combine it with a one-pointed attention at the same time. Detachment in reality *keeps* the abundance of the universe circulating in your life. If through the act of detachment, you feel you have lost something, then you truly do not understand the Law of Eternal Change.

My point is that anything you desire or want can be acquired through detachment, because it is based on *your own unquestionable belief in that power of your true-Self, the God-Self.*

The whole purpose of The Seven Laws of Nature philosophy is to help you '*experience*' being ultimately one with One-Self. This experience can only be described as an one in which you discover they are ultimately one in all things - as all things are one with them.

This universal oneness within One-Self may last only a few seconds when experienced as mind expansion – but its effect, even if experienced only once in a person's life-time, remains the major influence or criteria on 'identity-structure' in the individual.

All those who have felt it intuitively, do agree with me it is an experience where you have become one with stars, nature, all living things and the universe. I have personally experienced this ultimate universal Oneness within One-Self for the last twenty-five years, and I can tell you first hand it is real and has remained the major influence or criteria of the 'Identity-Structure' in my personality.

In a psychic nut-shell then The Law of Eternal Change works something like this: Everything in this universe must go through Change! Why? Because it's the law.

Through this Law, day changes into night, summer into winter, matter into energy, and energy into matter. A seed of an acorn changes into an oak tree. A seed of a rose blossoms into a flower. A child changes into an adult. The point to remember is that the only thing constant in this wholewide universe is change.

"How did The Seven Laws of Nature Surface?"

You are about to become acquainted with The Seven Laws of Nature which were revealed to me by an angel during the meditation sessions for helping me rebuild my own character. This experience has truly been one of the most cherished memories in my life. It has given me the opportunity to overcome the handicap of birth, being raised in an environment of the seven major enemies of all humankind namely: Fear, Hate, Jealousy, Superstition, Greed, Revenge and Anger.

This incident I want to share with you happened back in the fall of 1980, when I had regular sessions in sitting quietly, hoping for the creative ideas, which would help me overcome depression, anxiety, and feeling of self-pity due to a failure in a business venture in the Middle East.

I had lost everything that was precious to me: my home, belongings and business. Down on my luck and no place to go, I began to wander around searching for myself and some answers that would make my life bearable.

During the day, I spent much time in local parks and in public libraries, because they were free and warm. Hoping to find a royal road to riches and fortunes, I joined secret fraternal organizations. Day by day, I began to find myself sinking deeper and deeper into depression. I was totally broke: financially, emotionally and spiritually. And then, finally, out of depression I made some drastic changes. And the way I made these was that instead of feeling sorry for myself and blaming others for all my misfortunes, I deliberately assigned myself to the task of voluntary rebirth through the council meeting with my Creator God.

My purpose was to rebuild my own character, so it would represent the distilled wisdom of The Seven Laws of Nature philosophy, because these Laws represent God's thoughts. My passion, my mission, my obsession had become to discover how my life could become an expression of The Seven Laws of Nature, thus an expression of God's thoughts. This would be the essence of my own true-Self.

So every night over a long period of years, I held am imaginary council meeting with my true-Self, the God-Self! The procedure was this: just before going to sleep at night, when all my family was asleep, I would go to my walk-in closet upstairs next to my younger son's room where I would be undisturbed and alone.

I would sit quietly for about 15 minutes, trying to relax. I would have a few incenses burning in the closet where I sat quietly in a chair meditating. A fragrant odor and its smoke instantly put my mind in a state of relaxation and mystical absorption. Then I would shut my eyes and see, in my imagination, the presence of a higher power around me, while I held an imaginary council meeting with it.

Such meetings went a step beyond meditation, which involves the contemplation of an image; but mine was more than meditation. It was active imagination which brought into focus an image, voice, or figure of the unconscious, then entered into an interaction with me.

I was not passively watching, but was positively involved in what was happening. It is a version of the guardian angel or a manifestation of the Holy Spirit. If a relationship with this inner figure is developed, we are greatly helped. It is like having a psychologist or a spiritual director. In some cases, it is the way to access our unconscious wisdom.

Realizing as I did early in life, I had to overcome the handicap of birth: raised in an environment of the seven major negative emotions, I deliberately applied myself to the task of voluntary rebirth through the council meeting I shall describe below. My sessions with my Creator God would vary, according to my need for guidance for my problems at the moment. The procedure was exactly the same every night: going to my walk-in closet upstairs next to my younger son's room where I would be undisturbed and alone.

Here I had not only the opportunity to sit with the higher power in my imagination, but I actually dominated the council meeting by having a heart-to-heart talk with my Creator God.

I was astounded by the discovery that these imaginary meetings had become apparently real. It was not just meditation alone. It went beyond to active imagination. I was not passively watching, but was positively that involved in what was happening. Occasionally, it brought into focus an image, voice, or figure of the unconscious, which then entered into an interaction with me.

This is the first time I have had the courage to mention this. Heretofore, I have remained quiet on the subject, because I knew from my own attitude in connection with such matters I would be misunderstood if I described my unusual experience.

I have been emboldened now to reduce my experience to the printed page, because I am now less concerned about what "they say" than I was in the years that have passed.

You may accept or reject the information; the vital decision rests with you. But remember this is my true story, and I feel entitled to share it with all those who have an open mind in such matters.

I was astounded by the discovery that these imaginary council meetings with my Creator God had become very real.

One night about quarter past midnight, as I was indulging my imagination in my nightly council meetings, using an active imagination technique, I vividly saw what appeared to be an angel sitting quietly and writing something in a golden book. I sensed a brilliant, glowing white light, such a bright light only a short gaze was possible.

In my imagination, I asked the angel, "What are you writing about?"

He replied, "I am writing the names of all those whom God loves the most."

I asked, "Is my name written in that golden book?"

The angel looked and looked from the very first page to the last and said, "No." He repeated the answer by saying, "Your name is not mentioned anywhere in the golden book.

I then asked the angel, "Please put my name on the list of all those who loved mankind or humanity the most."

He said he would, and he did write it down e among the people on the list who loved mankind the most; then suddenly the angel vanished.

Having seen him face-to-face and being in that brilliant, bright glowing white light, I observed that while having this imaginary meeting with the angel, I was truly lifted to a higher level of mental stimulation.

It was indeed a "State-of-Mind" I cannot fully describe in a one volume book. Being touched by an angel instantly put me in a positive "State-of-Mind" where I experienced the sensation of being in control of my mind and body.

The conversation between myself and the angel, purely through my mind, was an experience where I could 'feel' or *assume* my Other-Self, the God-Self, and I could truly see through my physical body to my own true spiritual individuality.

The Seven Laws of Nature philosophy is based on the fact that each human being on this planet Earth has not one but TWO DISTINCT PERSONALITIES within himself or herself. One we see when we stand in front of a mirror. This physical personality is known as the "PERSONAL-SELF." This is the One that usually brings us misery, sickness, poverty, unhappiness and all the other BAD things of life we do not want or desire.

Then the other we NEVER see when we stand in front of a Mirror, but rather 'feel' or *assume* this new personality within us. This spiritual one is known as the "GOD-SELF," the "Self" that always brings us health, happiness, peace, and prosperity and *all* the other GOOD things of life we DO want and desire.

This is the 'Self" that lets us recognize within ourselves a greater potential and to use it to enrich the quality of our daily lives. This one is infinitely creative, infinitely loving and totally balanced. This one, *when* discovered, it fulfills consciousness.

A few throughout history have becomes 'saints' through this ultimate experience of their minds, but this is not the aim or goal. To live life more productively by greater participation in The Seven Laws of Nature, is the aim or goal. Truly, if all the world understood Nature's Laws to Successful Living, then lived-by-them indeed all the problems of the Earth would be solved.

One of the profound benefits I received by doing my nightly meditation using active imagination was that I actually began to 'experience' a universal oneness within myself. All those, who *have* 'experienced' this, intuitively agree with me. It is an 'experience' where you have become one with stars, nature, all thing living and the universe.

This 'experience' can only be described as one in which you will discovers that you are ultimately one with things as all things are one with you and discover everything in this whole universe is nothing more nor less than an '*energy*', including ourselves. We are all connected with each other through universal energy, and we somehow communicate with each other through this energy.

The revelation of this universal oneness within oneself may last only a few seconds when experienced as a mind expansion; its effect, even if experienced only *once* in a person's life-time, remains the major influence or criteria 'Identity-Structure' in the individual.

Speaking for myself, this has been the ultimate experience in my life, and I can honestly say it has been the major influence or criteria 'Identity-Structure' in my personal, professional and social life.

My encounter with my guardian angel has been another factor in reshaping my own life. The conversation, which took place between myself and the angel was purely through my mind. Since my eyes were closed, all thoughts came like a flood. The angel revealed each of The Seven Laws of Nature sequentially, one then another, as I indulged myself in my nightly active imagination.

During my twenty-five years of research and studies while putting the manuscript of the first edition of this book together, I also witnessed a scripture quotation from the parallel Bible in the book of Revelation 20:15, about the book-of-life (the golden book) in which contained the names of people who loved the most. I quote:

"…AND WHOSOEVER WAS NOT FOUND
WRITTEN IN THE BOOK OF LIFE
WAS CAST INTO THE LAKE OF FIRE."

I often wondered about the book-of-life the Bible spoke of as the same golden book I saw my angel writing the names of all people whom God loves the most. Most of my life, I truly believed the whole purpose of life is to serve mankind or humanity. I also believed that when we choose deeds and actions that bring happiness and success to others, we achieve true greatness, success and everything that comes with it.

That is why I had asked the angel to write down my names in the list of all those people who loved mankind or humanity the most. I reasoned that loving each other, helping each other in their needs, and serving other fellow human beings was probably more important than our mad rush to accumulate material things.

Apparently, this is *exactly* the right thing to do to please God the most.

I longed for the next moments when I would be in the presence of the same angel. I reasoned that when I saw the angel again, I would ask for the answers I was seeking to make my life bearable.

Several weeks went by, but I did not see that brilliant, bright, glowing light in my active imagination. But I somehow I knew I would meet the angel again, if I persisted in these nightly council meetings.

And then it happened!

About seven weeks later, as I was indulging my imagination in my regular nightly meetings, I saw the very same angel again.

This time he was sitting quietly with his wings gently beating and his left hand on the left page on the very first page of that golden book. He pointed to a name with his index finger and his eyes staring at the sky.

The angel seemed to be perplexed and pondered on something as he gazed at the page, as though not believing what he saw. I was curious to learn what was going on, so I walked toward the angel in my imagination and looked over his shoulder. As I gazed at the golden book, to my amazement I saw my name written on the top of the page among the list of all those people whom God regards with favor.

I then asked the angel, "How is it my name is listed at the top of the list of those people whom God loves the most?

The angel replied, "Your desire to love mankind or humanity pleased God the most. Your task is to build a better world."

I answered, "How? This world is such a large vast place, and, oh so complicated now. And I am so small and useless. There is nothing I could do."

But the angel in all his wisdom said, "You just build a better you."

I answered, "How?"

The angel smiled and said, "You have been chosen to receive The Seven Laws of Nature to share with others in the hope these laws will enrich their lives as they will yours.'

I then said, "Why me? I am nobody."

The angel paused for a few seconds. He was trying to find a gentle way to explain just why I was chosen for this task. He said when he saw my name listed on the top of the list of whom God loves the most, he was also perplexed. But the angel continued, God works in mysterious ways. We do not question his ways; we only obey his commands.

He said he had the privilege of being a guardian angel to hundreds of men and women, and he was always amazed every one of them were nobodies in the beginning, and they all became somebody as soon as they allowed these Natural Laws to dominate their lives.

He said this universe did not care if you are nobody. All it cares about is that you Learn, then <u>*live*</u> by these seven laws of nature. That's all.

I paused for a moment and began to show a look of doubt and skepticism on my face. The angel said, "What's the matter? Aren't you pleased that God loves you and wants you to have The Seven Laws of Nature to share them with others to make this world a better place in which to live.

I said hesitantly, "But who is going to believe me, listen to me or even read my book, if it is ever published. I am nobody."

The angel kept his silence and said nothing. I immediately continued by saying, "Most people in this world have their own religion. Furthermore, they are very partial to their own religious beliefs. How can I change or even attempt to influence these people?"

The angel, with all his God-given wisdom, smiled; after a brief pause he said, "It's true that most people in this world are very partial to their own religious beliefs, and no matter what you say, they will not allow any other metaphysical thinking to enter their minds. For example, A good Christen is a true follower of the teachings of the Holy Bible. Likewise, a true Muslim is a follower of the teachings of the Holy Quran. The same is true of the followers of Abraham's or Moses' one God.

"The point is that there are still millions of people in this world, who are not religious in the traditional sense, but these people are very spiritual. These are the ones who will be extremely interested in learning, then <u>*living*</u> by The Seven Laws of Nature.

So I asked the important question. "Why are there only Seven Laws of Nature?'

The angel replied that actually there are several hundred laws that govern and control this universe. Some laws deal with Mind, some with Soul and some with Life itself. If you endeavored to master all of them, it would probably take you a longer time than one lifetime.

However, there are only seven laws that open the door to your personal growth and fulfillment, the know-how for better living, and they will give you the key to joyful and prosperous living, the certain way to the only true genuine success.

Then, the angel concluded with the statement that I was chosen to share them with others in the hope the Seven Laws will enrich their lives as they will mine.

I shook my head in agreement and asked, "Tell me this. Why is it so important to teach these laws to highly spiritual people?"

The angel seemed pleased with my question, because he knew I was getting close to the truth and message he was trying so hard to convey to me.

The angel said, "There are several reasons why God wants you to receive The Seven Laws of Nature and more importantly to share them with the world. One of the main reasons is these Seven Natural Laws will propel people to a totally new spiritual cultural here on earth.

He continued, "During this new millennium, these spiritual human beings will begin to grasp these Laws sequentially, one after another. This will be the turning point in the lives of these highly spiritual people.

"Why?

"Because through the proper understanding of these Seven Natural Laws, then *living* by them, they will eventually find a pathway to true religion and eventually to the *acceptance* of one Creator God."

I said, "How do I start?"

The angel replied that I was to continue my nightly council meetings, and he would appear whenever he felt I was ready to receive them one-by-one.

So … what you have learned in the page of each and every chapter is a distilled wisdom of the ages, taught to me by my guardian angel during my nightly council meetings, so realistic that many times I became fearful of their consequences. These meetings were so real I would lose sight of the fact that my nightly meetings were purely the experiences of my imagination. The conversation took place between myself and the angel purely through my own mind.

Least I be misunderstood, I wish to state here most emphatically I still regard my council meetings as being purely imaginary, but I feel entitled to suggest that, while the angel may be fictional and the council meetings existent in my imagination, they have led me into glorious paths of adventure, rekindled an appreciation of true greatness, encouraged creative endeavor, and emboldened the expression of honest thought.

But the most important benefit I've received is the self-knowledge that revealed my unique and special talent as well as the purpose for which I was given the opportunity to live this life as a human being and depart from this world a more evolved soul.

START HERE

What greater benefit anyone can ask for?

This is the first time I have had the courage to mention this incident. Heretofore, I have remained quiet, because I knew from my own attitude in connection with such matters I would be misunderstood if I describe my unusual experience to others. I'm sharing this now, only to follow the command of my angel who was directed by a higher power to guide me.

If you too have had any encounter with the higher power or have ever been touched by an angel (real or imaginary), I would love to hear from you. Perhaps, we could share your experience with other members of our (IMS) society, and collectively help make this world a better world in which to live. (For ***free*** details about the trade paperback book).

Please write to:
Dr. Mushtaq H. Jaafri
P.O.Box 3698
San Dimas, California 91773
United States of America

Finally, I also want to make it perfectly clear I became aware of my TWO DISTINCT PERSONALITIES by reading a philosophy of individual achievements utilizing The Seven Laws of Nature, *but* the full account of These Laws was revealed to me during my meditation using active imagination. The conversation, which took place between myself and the angel happened purely through my own mind, was an experience where I could 'feel' or *assume* my Other-Self, the God-Self, and I could truly see through my physical body to my true spiritual individuality.

When you finish The Seven Laws of Nature, then *live-by-them,* I personally guarantee your knowledge of your true self will be much better than when you started. I guarantee it.

Applying The Law Of Eternal Change!

I will put The Law of Eternal Change into effect by making a commitment to take the following steps:

(1) I will accept each moment "As Is" – and NOT "As-It-Should-Be." I will also accept each individual person, whether it by my spouse, my child, my close friend or a business associate, as he or she is – and NOT as he or she should be. I'll welcome new changes in life during each day, week, month or year.

(2) I will thank God for the understanding of The Seven Laws of Nature, thus enabling me to understand myself. I *affirm* this truth to myself daily. This understanding will help me recognize and assimilate the TWO DISTINCT PERSONALITIES within me. Because of this "Self-knowledge," I will eventually see through my physical body to my own true spirituality.

(3) I will remember that nature leads human beings through CHANGE or Struggle by peaceful means as long they cooperate, but nature resorts to revolutionary methods if we rebel and neglect or refuse to conform to The Law of Eternal Change. And instead of crying out in rebellion or shivering

> with fear, I will hold my head high and look in all direction for the 'seed' of an equivalent benefit in every circumstance of CHANGE or Struggle or Sorrow, for these are the God-given Laws. I'll share this book with one more person. I'll help build a lasting bond and rapport with others. I'll help make America strong and wealthy, <u>ONE-PERSON-AT-A-TIME.</u> I will help make this world a better place to live.

Summary And Conclusion!

Let me sun up everything we have covered so far by telling you a little story.

A beautiful radiant butterfly floats gently through the trees in a deep-carpeted forest.

It lights upon a golden flower, its wings softly beating. It lays its eggs upon a leaf, which will hatch into a tiny and ugly caterpillar, who does not know it has the talent of becoming a gorgeous butterfly. It springs a strong sturdy cocoon. True! The cocoon protects it, but also imprisons it. The caterpillar will never be a beautiful butterfly until it breaks the bonds of its prison, one that it made for itself. Eventually, the caterpillar frees itself and becomes the gorgeous butterfly. You, as the active participant in this new cultural transformation in human society, using The Seven Nature's Laws to Successful Living have already taken a giant step toward freeing yourself, toward living up to your full potential. Let me give you a brief preview of what you can expect to gain when you start applying The Seven Laws of Nature, moving from the role of a mere learner to one of a teacher.

The very First Law of Nature compares the Mind with the solar system of the universe, shows you how to control the Mind by simply fixing your own dominating thoughts towards the mental picture or images of your aim or goal in life.

The Second Law of Nature reveals the means by which your Mind becomes a connecting link between MIND and Nature and to that greater power available in the universe, which is our privilege to harmonize with.

The Third Law of Nature deals with a miracle, which contains a PASSWORD capable of making you free and helping you appropriate all the great riches of life, such as lasting friendships, harmonious family relationships, sympathy, and understanding business associates, and inner harmony which brings peace of mind measurable only in spiritual values. The riches within your grasp cannot always be measured in money. The philosophy of *The Seven Laws of Nature* will prepare you to attract and enjoy these higher states which always have been and always will be denied to all except *those who are ready for them.*

The Fourth Law of Nature shows you a unique new success formula in action, which may make it possible for you to *condition* or program your MIND for success, using a higher power of God. This new success formula consists of the understanding of a cardinal truth:

"the good you do for others sets into motion the good in God's mind, which returns to you many times over in the good you receive from others."

The Fifth Law of Nature opens the door to the temple of wisdom known as the sixth sense. This Law leads you toward the full and complete understanding of your own true-Self, the God-Self, which you don't normally see when you stand before a mirror. Be prepared, when you begin to put the philosophy of *The Seven Laws of Nature* into action, for a changed life which will not only ease the trials and stress of living, but will also prepare you for the accumulation of material riches in abundance.

The Sixth Law of Nature asks the most important questions that will surely help you find your purpose or perhaps mission in life, and it will guide you step-by-step and show you how to accomplish it. Ask yourself, "Who Am I?" and "What our existence really means?"

Answer these two questions truthfully, and you'll have given your life a new direction.

The Seventh Law of Nature is the apex of this philosophy. It is very short and in general. It can be assimilated, understood and applied only by first mastering the other six. You and I are very special people, because we are trying to start a new spiritual cultural transformation in human society. It's a kind of renaissance in consciousness, occurring very slowly. It's not religious in nature, but spiritual, and you will discover something new about human life on this planet, about what our existence means, and how it will eventually alter human culture dramatically.

The Seven Laws of Nature are an original and systematic attempt to mark out a new and important field of human knowledge. These Laws will affirm that you can have the best lifeoffers. These Nature's Laws to Successful Living will show humanity how to LIVE...BE...AND HAVE THE BEST. Successful living and being and having is based upon the knowledge of, and obedience to The Seven Laws of Nature.

This is a remarkable achievement for just one volume. Yet all these benefits are yours when you make a commitment to start applying The Seven Laws of Nature in your life and share them with someone else, perhaps your spouse, your child, your close friend, your business associate. Do it soon while it is still fresh in your own mind. You'll surely notice the difference in your mental and emotional process.

Those you teach will see you as a changing, growing person and will be more inclined to be helpful and supportive as you work perhaps together to integrate The Seven laws of Nature into your lives. By applying Them on a daily basis, you'll eventually learn to know yourself to the degree where certain unconscious elements of the super-conscious Mind (Mind of Nature) become ONE with you. You'll thus experience yourself as being one with stars, nature, all things living and the universe.

As you begin work on The Seven Laws of Nature philosophy, I would suggest three mind-set shifts that will greatly increase the benefits you will receive from this material.

First, when you read this volume, read IF I were your personal friend and writing to you and YOU alone. This way, you'll sense my presence while reading the material.

Second, I would suggest you shift your mind-set of your involvement in this material from the role of mere learner to that of a teacher. Take the panoramic view, and read with the purpose of sharing or discussing what you learned with one more person.

Third, whether you believe that the author actually had an angelic experience, or think it is purely fictional is of no concern here. "Everything that enlarges the sphere of human powers, that shows man he can do what he though he could not do, is valuable," said one of the greatest thinkers of this world, Ben Johnson. If you follow the above three mind-set shift suggestions in spirit as well as action, you'll surely be rewarded with a form of riches sufficient to give you a well-balanced life.

"The great end of life is NOT knowledge, but action," Thomas Huxley said. "Don't find fault, find remedy," said the immortal Henry Ford. You'll achieve freedom from all fears and the peace-of-mind, which shall endure and ease the trials and stress of living, while preparing you for the accumulation of all material riches in abundance.

Love and joy will flood your soul. The problems and the struggles of your life will evaporate through the proper understanding and use of nature's secrets. The outside affairs of the world are all immaterial to you when you learn to live from within by applying The Seven Laws of Nature on a daily basis. But mostly the three mind-set shift suggestions will encourage your own MIND to get the most value and benefit from the things that follow.

All right! What follow?

As you begin to understand all The Seven Laws of Nature, you will begin to focus on your true purpose in life, which will lead you to two big questions.

(1) "Who am I?"
(2) "What can I do in this world?"

Through the application of The Seven Laws of Nature, you'll learn the genius of nature's intelligence. These are the *THOUGHTS OF GOD* – the rest are just details.

One of world's greatest mathematicians and scholars, Albert Einstein, use to say, "I want to know God's thoughts … the rest are details." I often wonder if he wasn't referring to The Seven Laws of Nature.

One of the most amazing things you'll learn is that YOU too have a purpose in life — or a unique gift — or a special talent to give to others. A talent so great that only YOU can do it best.

And you too can express your unique and special talent and fulfill the needs of your fellow human beings. You begin to create whatever you want, whenever you want it.

Soon you'll discover that your life too has become an expression of God's thoughts. This will be the essence of your true-Self. The whole purpose of this philosophy is to help you utilize more of your potentials and to free you from the bondage of all the self-imposed limitations, which have imprisoned you for so long and to allow you to become the beautiful, radiant, butterfly GOD intended for you to be.

If you are like any human being I know, you too are searching for solutions to problems and you can use some help.

Like all of us, you tried many avenues, sought advice from many people, and yet most of the problems remain.

Well – WE BELIEVE IN YOU! We believe the solution to ANY problem in any area of your life exists within YOU! As you gain experience with The Seven Laws of Nature by sharing this philosophy with others, whether it be your spouse, your child, your close friend or a business associate, you'll learn this is so.

In the meantime, I know no one likes to face problems and troubles alone. Friends and relatives can sometimes offer short term help just by being there and by listening, but you must remember they have their own worries, their own unresolved problems.

As a staff member of the (IMS) International Mind-Conditioning Society, you can be certain that every other member, including our directors, understands you and has compassion and can offer support while you are in the process of finding your answers to the riddle of life.

As the popular slang expression goes, "WE KNOW WHERE IT'S AT." Why? Because we have been there. We all have bruises and scars from it. JUST AS YOU HAVE.

You are NOT alone. Every member of this cultural transformation society is dedicated to helping you help yourself. When you have become a member for some time, you too will feel and profit from the same dedication. MEN AND WOMEN OF ALL AGES AND RELIGIOUS BELIEFS ARE WELCOME! Especially those people in the golden years who are needed to help and support the young ones.

In closing, let me say this:

You have the greatest gift that anyone on earth could have – THE GIFT OF LIFE ITSELF, a precious gift from our Creator, and what we make of life is our gift back to our Creator. The amazing thing is that so many of us erect our own prison and LOCK ourselves in. We construct the highest walls around ourselves. Maximum security. No one can penetrate those walls. No one can get to us. We feel secure, but after a while we feel bored.

We get tired getting up in the morning, going to bed at night, going through the same routine – year after year – really going nowhere. Then we begin to rebel. We want out – the walls we erected to keep others out keeps us from getting out. We feel stifled; we feel enraged. We forgot the prison is of our own creation. No one put up the walls, which forbade us from going out; no one put up the walls, but ourselves. We rage and fume, forgetting where we hid the KEY.

So – if we do not find the KEY – which is within ourselves all along, we remain a prisoner of our own self-imposed limitations and restrictions. Please believe me when I tell you the KEY you'll find within The Seven Laws of Nature, and the three mind-set shift suggestions will literally change your own life for the better just as surely it has mine and all those who applied the Nature's Laws to Successful Living.

This 'Self-knowledge' can and will turn your MIND around 180 degrees, from failure to success – from rejections to friendship – from timidity to self-confidence – from self-conscious to self-esteem.

Do you have problems that defy solutions?

I mean business problems, money problems, people problems, and marriage problems. Then you'll want to read this amazing new book time after time, whenever you are faced with a problem or a difficult decision, or whenever you happen to be in the midst of your sorrow, struggles and you need to make a new fresh start.

If you are in the middle of sorrows that are unbearable, ones that are insurmountable, and you feel a need for a change in life, then The Seven Laws of Nature philosophy will be an enormous help to you in strengthening your decisions.

If you want to reduce stress in your life or eliminate tension completely, get-rid of nervousness that causes most major illness, or if you just want to control all negative thoughts and emotions, then this book is a must reading for you. If you want to have a calm, relaxed attitude at all times, or simply peace-of-mind and better health, or to control your anger, fear, excitement or heart attack, then you just can't afford to take The Seven Laws of Nature lightly.

This amazing new book represents the 'Self-knowledge', the 'Know-how', the distilled wisdom of the ages as revealed to me by my guardian angel over a quarter of a century ago. It has thus been nearly thirty years in preparation.

S0 – you'll have all this wealth of 'Self-knowledge' behind you if you are willing to learn, then, *live* by The Seven Laws of Nature. By the time you teach others either individually or in a group, everything will fall in place. It is at this point you begin to understand your true-Self, the God-Self.

Moreover, it is at this point you can truly understand the holy quotation:

"AS A MAN OR WOMAN THINKETH OR BELIEVETH IN HIS OR HET HEART – SO IS HE OR SHE."

Now – you WILL succeed, because you know you WILL. You will master each Law, step by step, because it is organized incrementally. You will shift the mind-set of your own involvement in this material from the role of a mere learner to that of a teacher.

You will take your time and read this material with the purpose of sharing and discussing what you learn with someone else. You will read this material as though you are going to teach it to your spouse, your child, your close friend, your business associate today or perhaps in a week while it is still fresh in your mind. Notice the difference in your mental and emotional processes.

You'll soon be pleasantly surprised by what appears to be "A NEW YOU" emerging from your self-made Cocoon. But you know something? It's NOT a new YOU at all. It's simply the new YOU, which you never allowed to be released before. It's the YOU that thought you could not relax – could not solve any problems – could not be happy – could not be wealthy. One of the main reasons you thought you could not is because most of your life people have been telling you, YOU CAN'T DO IT. YOU CAN'T HAVE IT. YOUCAN'T BE ANYBODY.

So –you in turn have found it easy to slip into the habit of saying to yourself, "I CAN'T DO IT." or "I CAN'T HAVE IT." or "I CAN'T BE THAT." instead of saying to yourself, "I CAN, I CAN, I CAN," perhaps a million times.

But can you really do it?

You always think you know the odds against succeeding, but do you think the odds are in favor of succeeding. ***One last word***: You are not a failure simply because you are not wealthy at present or do not own a fancy car or a big home.

BUT YOU ARE A FAILURE, IF YOU NOW DO NOT BEGIN TO DEVELOP THE VAST POTENTIALS WITHIN YOU! You must try to do your level best to reach whatever reasonable goals you have in your life.

So long for now, my good friend.

You certainly have come a long way. You should be congratulated. YOU, my friend, do have a very real purpose in life, for which only YOU were chosen to give to the world. This purpose mainly deals with service to humanity. You do have a unique talent to give to others. And when you blend this unique talent with service to others, you experience the ecstasy and exultation of your own spirit, which is the ultimate goal of all goals.

I wish I might feel privileged to tell you just what you'll find as your purpose or mission in life or your unique and special talent. But that would definitely deprive you of much of the benefit you'll receive when you make the discover in your own way. I'm not making you guess, really, but telling you these things outright might ruin the surprise, and you wouldn't be given the boost you need to get started on your way. I'm going to give you a little shove in the right direction.

May I suggest you consider becoming a charter member of the new cultural transformation society, known as (IMS) or International Mind-Conditioning Society – for, this will surely push you in the right direction. I guarantee it!

You are cordially invited!

Please consider allowing yourself the privilege of joining me personally in an International movement in human society. It's not religious in nature, but spiritual. More information is available from the author on the ideas brought forth in *The Seven Laws of Nature.* You may also subscribe to a monthly newsletter written by the author entitled *"An Awakening"* which chronicles his present experiences and reflections on the new spiritual awakening occurring on our planet.

This newsletter is aimed at helping you understand your own true-Self, the God-Self and discovering your most inspired, spiritual mission in life, which mainly deals with service to mankind or humanity, as well as helping you to connect with the *energy* available in the universe. An open mind and a willingness to belong to a group of spiritual people are needed to start a new cultural transformation in human society. This goal will be accomplished through writings for friendship, encouragement, and spiritual and moral support. We would like to hear from anyone – beginners or accomplished writers - to contribute their unique and special talent through this newsletter. Reply by mail with qualifications. Your confidentiality is guaranteed.

Or at the very least …stay in touch with me personally by writing me now and telling me what The Seven Laws of Nature philosophy did for you and how it has changed your own life for the better. I would greatly appreciate it. But I can promise you if you will allow me the privilege of coaching you and of working with me personally, I'll assist you in taking whatever changes you make by participating in The Seven Laws of Nature philosophy, which will take you to an even greater level of success and fulfillment than you ever imagined.

Are You Ready For Part Two?

The Seven Laws of Nature, (Part Two) series is especially written for those who have ***not*** yet discovered the TWO DISTINCT PERSONALITIES within us. To be sure of discovering your two distinct personalities, you must overcome one more hurdle. It deals with programming the MIND with The Seven Laws of Nature.

By creating the world's first, innovative concept of using a *flow chart* similar to those used to devise computer programs, Dr. Jaafri shows us how we can train our minds to embrace the positive forces (even as we eliminate all negative emotions), so that every individual can gain *access* to the cosmic flow of abundance.

In the Part Two series, you'll discover just how each law of nature comes into surface, so you can be ready and prepared to implement these positive forces and to recognize and assimilate two "selves" (the physical and spiritual). This is an enthusiastic and inspirational self-help book.

One Last Comment

One of my most cherished goals in life is to establish an International Mind-Conditioning Society (IMS), where people from all over the world come to attend sessions in "Sitting For Creative Ideas." I envision this as a world-wide networking organization, where men and women of all ages and religious beliefs meet together to discuss how they can achieve their own goals without anyone criticizing or discouraging.

Participation in this society is absolutely free. To join, all you need do is send your name, address and, if you like, your phone number to:

Dr. Mushtaq H. Jaafri
Box 3698, San Dimas, California, 91773 USA.

**OPPORTUNITY
BOOK
BONANZA**

"A TOUCH OF GREATRNESS." By Frank Tibolt

This award-winning book could be worth a million dollars to you, this book teaches the moneymaking "Secrets That Can Change Your Life. "Based on author's famed "600+ Tips" and (12) lessons action program. For self-advancement multiply your thinking power with thinking alphabet. **MP-3 ……. (Available in soft paperback cover only)**

Retail Price $19.95 ………………. Internet Shopper Price $8.95 Plus $1 shipping

"THE SEVEN LAWS OF NATURE." By Dr. Mushtaq H. Jaafri

This award-winning book is written for "those who have done all right in life" to guide them on the path to full realization of their goals. Applying the precepts of this approach will put you on the fast track to true success and becoming the person you want to be. Based on author's famed angelic revelations. **MJ-5 ….(Soft trade paperback cover)**

Retail Price $19.95 ………………. Internet Shopper Price $8.95 Plus $1 shipping

"THE MIND-CONDITIONING SYSTEM" Part One and Part Two.

By Dr. Mushtaq H. Jaafri. (Special 8 1/2 x11 edition.)

A two volume course that teaches an original, cutting-edge technology for getting beyond self-limiting negative emotions and thoughts. This book uses a computer-like flow chart to reprogram the mind, just as computer is reprogrammed. Readers learn how to take any negative emotion and turn it into a positive emotion to set them free to achieve peace-of-mind…success and happiness. Part One also teaches how to sell information by mail order and make money. **MC-12 … (Soft trade paperback cover available in hard copy.)**

Retail Price $20.00 Each Volume…Internet Shopper Price…$19.95 for both Volumes.

SAVE ……. $46.00 …….ORDER ALL FOUR BOOKS ………

Special Offer for the Internet Shopper. Buy all four books (Hard Copies by Mail) and pay only $33.00. We will pay shipping and handling.

Mail Your Order To:

Mushtaq Publishing Company
P.O. Box 3698
San Dimas, CA 91773

What Do You Think?
Tell Us and Win a Gift!

We want each edition of this ebook to be as useful and helpful as possible. To achieve this goal, we need to know what you liked, what you didn't care for, and what additional information you want us to include.

Completed feedback sheets will be entered in a contest to win a $20.00 book plus FREE current Copy of the Newsletter *"An Awakening"*, which chronicles author's present experiences and reflections on the new spiritual awakening occurring on planet Earth.

What are your favorite three Laws? ______________________
Why?____

What are your least favorite three Laws?__________________
Why?____

What did you think was the most valuable lesson you learned in this book? ____

What other information you want to read about that wasn't included in this book?

____

Would you share these Laws with someone else whether it be your spouse, your child, friend or a business associates?

____

To enter the contest, simply complete the form below.

Name:____

Street Address:____

City: ________________ **State:**_______ **Zip Code:**__________

Mail Completed form to:
Dr. Mushtaq H. Jaafri (Dept. Contest)
P.O. BOX 3698
San Dimas, CA 91773

About the Author

Dr. Mushtaq H. Jaafri was born in Sialkot City, Pakistan, a land that has produced many scholars, poets, and deep-thinking people. He came to the United States a foreign student in search of self-knowledge and the meaning of life and purpose. He received his doctoral degree in the science of metaphysics from the University of Metaphysics in Los Angeles, California. He is an author and a publisher, a teacher and a public speaker. He is a founder of the *International Mind-Conditioning Society*, an organization devoted exclusively to the teaching of the working principles of the human mind. His life goal is to establish a scientific laboratory where people from all over the world come to exchange creative ideas. If you are interested, please write.

www.ingramcontent.com/pod-product-compliance
Ingram Content Group UK Ltd.
Pitfield, Milton Keynes, MK11 3LW, UK
UKHW040601210726
13854UKWH00008B/1669

9 781403 306111